Women

Who

Make

a Fuss

Isabelle Stengers & Vinciane Despret

—————————— and collective ——————————

Françoise Balibar, Bernadette Bensaude-Vincent, Laurence Bouquiaux, Barbara Cassin, Mona Chollet, Emilie Hache, Françoise Sironi, Marcelle Stroobants, Benedikte Zitouni

translated by April Knutson | Univocal

Les faiseuses d'histoires
Que font les femmes à la pensée ?
by Isabelle Stengers, Vinciane Despret & collective
© Editions La Découverte, Paris, France, 2011

Translated by April Knutson
as *Women Who Make a Fuss:*
The Unfaithful Daughters of Virginia Woolf

First Edition
Minneapolis © 2014, Univocal Publishing

Published by Univocal
123 North 3rd Street, #202
Minneapolis, MN 55401

Designed & Printed by Jason Wagner

Distributed by the University of Minnesota Press

ISBN 9781937561192
Library of Congress Control Number 2014933006

TABLE OF CONTENTS

WOMEN WHO MAKE A FUSS:

THE UNFAITHFUL DAUGHTERS OF VIRGINIA WOOLF

PART ONE

1

WE WHO ARE AT THE UNIVERSITY

We are among those women who entered the university certainly knowing that not everyone (male or female) would be allowed entrance, but without really thinking about the fact that, as girls, we posed a particular question. One quickly forgets the history, once a right is acquired and one is living in the general conditions permitting one to benefit from that right. If we wanted it, if we were "good" enough, and if we were lucky, we could even have an academic career.... In short, the question of the democratization of access to the university could surely be posed, and was, moreover, but it didn't concern us specifically, "as women."

Naturally, we could have posed this question again at a certain moment of our journey, when statistics began to show that, at the university as in many other places, careers differed noticeably according to whether one was a man or a woman (and especially if one was a woman who had a child). And today, in one way or another, we can think that these statistics speak about us: even though both of us have "made a career," why is neither one of us a full professor? Had we been blocked by what is called the "glass ceiling," this sort of invisible boundary which, on average, men may cross over whereas it blocks the careers of women with an equivalent diploma? The explanations that take into account this invisible boundary are not lacking: first of all, the massively unequal division of family duties, not to mention a host of little differences that we bear witness to ourselves, but which, for us, were not worthy of making a lot of fuss over.

We were no exception in feeling unconcerned. Both the strength and the weakness of statistics reside in what they show and what they ignore. They aggregate but engage only with difficulty, for many women can recount their career path while justifying its stagnation, even speaking of a "choice" in the matter. Why have they made or had to make this choice, and why was no one else surprised or worried by it? Such questions are only actively posed when the institution suddenly considers women as a "resource" that it has not sufficiently exploited. Today, the weak recruitment in the science departments (the so-called "true" or sound sciences of the laboratory) has forced responsible people to make inquiries. They can no longer ignore the part of the fish tank which the future of research depends upon. It is thus a question of getting "girls" interested in careers which they seem to distance themselves from, only because of erroneous representation. The self-exclusion of girls would bear witness only to their belief that such careers are not for them because, as is well known, science is open to everyone, male or female, and is particularly neutral with regard to gender.

But both of us chose philosophy, and we have not felt that "it wasn't for us"—at least as women. If we had doubts, we didn't feel them on a political level, but a personal one. We pursued our studies, both of us having had the good fortune to find a stable position in a university philosophy department, and our writings have made us known. Admittedly, we know that, our works are not referenced in our profession, in the sense that citing them does not help those who cite them to

14

be recognized as true philosophers. We are not naive; we know that for certain men (and women!) our topics are suspect, or susceptible to dishonoring philosophy. Hypnosis, addicts, witches, the Arabian babbler, peasants, the uneasy dead ... problems that are neither serious nor conventional, as we had little interest in taking them as pretexts in order to score a point against other philosophers—or if we did, it was in order to create just enough space to allow ourselves to try to address our research topics. Each of us could then elicit a sigh: "so this is what she comes with!"

Neither one of us, however, is able to claim that what we have done (our choice of subjects as well as our manner of writing about them), we have done—or dared to do—because we were women. We worked this way because we imagined that philosophy should be done this way as well, because this is what we hoped for it to be: it was in doing philosophy this way that we showed that it was possible. At no moment did we envisage that doing philosophy this way could designate us as "women philosophers." Most of all we did it because this freedom of movement, for us, was the good fortune of philosophers.[1]

We say "was" because we are aware that the kind of freedom that we took for granted could, in the future, easily become impossible or suicidal, at least for those who are contemplating a university career. Today, something is happening that no longer has anything to do with statistics. In multiple ways, the same message now reverberates: "The party is over." Not that it was ever a party, properly speaking, of course, but the mobilizing enterprises always need to describe what they put an end to, emphasizing their unwarranted privileges, irresponsible laxity, and self-satisfied mediocrity. Competition and the will to excel that allow for survival are today officially on the agenda as unavoidable

---

1. The way we characterize philosophy, and will later characterize the university, refers to the situation in our (French speaking) part of Europe.

15

imperatives. Violence no longer only characterizes the relationships among competitors, but also the means of evaluation to which they must all submit. At every level, realism, the necessity to respond to demand (universities must produce useful knowledge and be competitive), the responsibility or the duty for everyone to make one's attractiveness quotient and one's capital prosper coexists in impunity with the eternal evocation of what the university is supposed to represent, "knowledge for knowledge's sake," progress, the Enlightenment. Knowledge worthy of this name must not fear evaluation, they say to us, and this evaluation must be objective: how many articles, published in which journals? How many contracts? How many collaborations with other prestigious institutions, thus contributing to the "positioning" of the university in the European or global market? This is the time for excellence, and in our field, where one cannot show one's worth by patenting results and/or by forging alliances with the industry, what is henceforth measured in the name of excellence now requires anyone who wants to "work as a philosopher" to be published in high impact, specialized journals read only by philosophers.

We have the impression of helplessly bearing witness to the end of an epoch, one where we could be delighted in seeing young women (and young men as well) acquire a taste for research and venture out wherever their questions would lead them—that is, to become capable of this freedom which we have both profited from. Must we from now on say to them: "Your efforts are an investment, look for orientations that are fashionable, ones that give access to A-rated journals?" One could retort that there is nothing there to make a fuss about, because what awaits them is not worse than what awaits all workers. Let us say then that the university is on the cusp of achieving "democratization." There, as everywhere else, it is going to be a question of being on guard to demonstrate one's flexibility, to learn to give good signals and to listen to those which come from the market. In short: to give the requisite guarantees of motivation and seriousness. And what is striking is that we, academics, have not been able to resist any better than the more vulnerable workers. We knew perfectly well that we were under attack but everyone seems to have thought that if s/he was clever enough, good enough, s/he would be able to escape the worst. Now we see converted colleagues manifesting a great loyalty to the new standard, firmly shouldering the role of guard-dogs against escapist temptations.

There may well be a connection between this lack of resistance to what is making us fall in line and the way in which, for several decades, universities have "endured" what is called their democratization. It can be said that the university merely put up with the arrival of "newcomers," for whom university knowledge is not their just due, but rather an adventure to an unknown land—first: the arrival of girls, next: youth from "less privileged" classes, and then: immigrants. If there was a collective preoccupation, it has not been the transformation of the arrival of young people who were not pre-formatted "heirs" into a dare, by offering them knowledge that would be worthy of them, or that which would open horizons other than that of joining the "elite" as it has been defined without them or even against them. Rather, the preoccupation has been the threat of a "lowering of the standard." You are welcome and your presence is normal, for we are "democrats," but on our terms, so that nothing changes. You are welcome as long as you do not make a fuss....

To make this connection is to avoid transforming us, who are at the university into innocent victims, or worse, into emblematic figures of disinterested and fruitful "true" knowledge, that "our enemies" would destroy because such knowledge disgusts them. This would really be giving us too much credit, all the more so because our institutions did not surrender after a desperate struggle, but rather readily accepted the necessary actions to be taken with the zeal of the newly converted. One can dream of an institution capable of resisting the injunction to submit "like everyone else" to the categorical imperatives of the market, but such a dream can hardly be dissociated from the dream of an institution that would have confronted (like a test required to prove its dignity) the necessity to examine the difference between routine work and the transmission and cultivation of "living knowledge" capable of nourishing the appetites and questions of the young men and women who come from elsewhere. But let us not dream. Let us accept the question now forced upon us: how do we live the end of this epoch in a manner that is neither cynical nor nostalgic? How do we avoid the rule today of "everyone for himself?"

"We who are at the university." Who is this "we?" What if the possibility of not succumbing to cynicism or nostalgia was at stake in this question, by way of the creation of a "we" who could learn to think together under duress and grant this duress the power to situate itself? A "we" who could learn to "make a fuss," capable of transforming what begins as personal disarray or plaintive nostalgia into a strength?

If we have learned to write collaboratively, on a theme which neither of us had tackled before, it is first of all to take on, thanks to the other, a creative process like this. And if we have been able to envision doing this, it is because we have experienced the possibility and the meaning of this creation. We owe this experience to an encounter with a "woman who made a fuss," with a woman that made a big fuss about what seemed to be a rather banal request. And for us, this encounter has constituted a test, calling for and demanding a strength very different from that which a rather abstract "we" invokes, uniting those who "all together" would defend research and prevent the market from enslaving the university.

It is a test to read *Three Guineas* by Virginia Woolf,[2] a work of resistance at the limit of despair. This book was published in 1938, while the war in Spain was in the process of ending in horror and terror, and while Hitler, having swallowed Austria whole, was turning his appetite toward Czechoslovakia. *Three Guineas* is a long response to a letter—to three letters in fact—but its point of departure and its final answer deal with the question which was addressed to her by the first letter: "How are we to prevent war?"[3] Her correspondent suggested that she sign a manifesto committing herself to "protect culture and intellectual freedom."[4]

We know the end of the story, an end which proved wrong all who, numerous at that time, thought that they could "prevent the war." For a time, the Munich agreement, as dishonorable as it was, allowed people to hope, but it was revealed to be a deception. "Munich appeaser" has become an insult in our time. But the answer of Virginia Woolf is not inscribed at this moment of hesitation. She is going to refuse to sign the manifesto, not because she thought that the war was (sadly) inevitable, but because she refused any loyalty to her country and to the ideals it defended. Scandalously, she dared to propose to her sisters that they not commit themselves to the side of their fathers and brothers, these "educated men" who called on them to defend their world.

2. We would not have encountered Virginia Woolf in this way without the intercession of Maria Puig de la Bellacasa, whom we will discuss later, and without the manner in which other researchers, associated like Maria with the Group of Constructivist Studies (GECo), continued her work and opened it toward other horizons. We take up the baton, joyful to be able to say that we owe them so much.

3. Virginia Woolf, *Three Guineas* (New York: Harcourt, Brace and Company, 1938), p. 3.

4. *Ibid.*, p. 129.

2

NOT IN OUR NAME

We are conscious of the fact that for certain women with whom we work and think such an answer is intolerable, even more so considering that intellectual freedom was of course essential to Woolf herself, and that she knew very well that she was, for the Nazis, a hateful and contemptible example of the corrupt world they intended to destroy. How could she refuse to become involved when they threatened not only the freedom of thought but also the vocation of women to think? *KKK, Kinder, Küche, Kirche,* does this not sum up the Nazi program for women?

It is not a question of judging, of declaring who's right and who's wrong, of justifying or excusing. If Virginia Woolf's answer has a meaning for us, it is not because of an analogy between her epoch and ours, but because such an analogy, sewn out of whole cloth, has been used in a rather obscene manner. We have heard people talk about "Munich appeasers," not only during the two Iraq wars, but also when it is a question of "defending our values" against a cowardly relativism which would lead, through a spirit of misplaced tolerance, to shameful accommodations. Nothing, as we have heard, will convince us to compromise the heritage that is the Enlightenment.

And this led us to read the letter that Virginia received a little differently. Did its author really believe that his manifesto for "culture and intellectual freedom" could contribute to the effort to prevent the threat of war? Perhaps the question isn't very interesting. What strikes us, rather, is the vacuity, that is to say the consensual character of the commitment demanded by this manifesto. It is evidently drawn up to assemble "good people" who do not want war but who will also not compromise their values. It seems to us that this kind of manifesto typically arises from initiatives precursory to a mobilization, when it is not yet possible to designate as "traitors" those who refuse the harsh necessity to declare war, but already brandish the standard of values that will unfortunately make that war necessary.

Virginia Woolf did not say no to the war, in the sense militant pacifists of the epoch did. But she refused to allow what she valued, that which was dearer to her than life, to become the standard for that war, as if a State could enter into a war for "intellectual freedom." If the war occurs, don't present it "in the name of our values," a war of good against evil. And most of all, don't make war "in our name!" This cry, "not in our name!" is the cry of men and women who refuse to see what is dear to them mobilized by their enemies. It resonated in the United States in 2002 when Bush used the pain of September 11th to justify the invasion of Iraq. *Not in our name will you wage endless war.* And it was reprised in 2004, on the occasion of International Women's Day, by the network *nextgenderation*: "To the new crop of self-proclaimed 'guardians of women's rights,' whom we have never encountered as participants or supporters of our women's movements and struggles over many years, we say determined: NOT IN OUR NAMES! Their cynical use of 'women's emancipation' and 'the equality of men and women' is as appalling as it is inveracious.

As feminists and women truly concerned with women's emancipation, we will not allow them to use the 'emancipation of women' for anti-immigrationist, assimilationist, islamophobic, and ethnocentric politics."[1]

We will not side with those who affirm that we must defend our values in the face of veiled women, women who wear the Burka, but also against those men and women who contest Darwinian evolution—that well-thinking persons are gathering to defend his theory would certainly have surprised Darwin. This time the cry is raised against those men (and women!) who shamelessly transform what was the object of long and difficult struggles into a synonym of consensual progress: the "heritage of the Enlightenment." And who could forget, with just as much tranquility, that it is not sufficient to "recognize" rights. Will well-thinking men rejoin the women in our countries for whom the struggle continues? "We must struggle against the violence of neoliberal politics—promoted to the rank of 'inescapable truths' of the free market—which demolish all the foundations of a real social security and which lead to a continual precariousness in our lives. We need to struggle against structural and everyday sexism, racism, and homophobia that we encounter in our lives, and we need all the alliances necessary to carry out these struggles. We need to struggle against the ways in which women are represented and are not—in our political and economic systems, in the dominant culture and media, in advertising. We need to struggle against the systematic reduction of the necessary resources for a politics of emancipation and against the closing of spaces that allowed us to develop our feminist politics."

Beyond instrumentalization, it is the capacity for amnesia that this instrumentalization presupposes which makes us dizzy. As if the rights of women or homosexuals had fallen from the tree of our civilization like a ripe apple. If one day we succeed in obtaining

---

1. This manifesto can be found online at http://nextgenderation.collectifs.net.

a peaceful and intelligent relationship regarding illegal drugs who will remember, the violent pressure placed on their consumers as well as on those regions of the world that for a long time have cultivated hashish, poppies, and cocoa?

The men and women today who appropriate the accomplishments of struggles in which they have not participated will perhaps protest that this is irrelevant, that such an analogy with addicts is offensive to women and homosexuals. And they would no doubt protest in a similar fashion, if we spoke to them of animals reduced to meat on paws. But tomorrow, perhaps, the amnesiac norm of progress will embrace addicts and animals and add them to the awards list of what our "grandeur" bears witness to.

Beyond the differences, it is perhaps the connection between the struggle against this amnesia and the capacity to resist, to think against the consensus, that traces a continuity between Woolf and those women today who say "not in our name."[2] For Virginia Woolf didn't just refuse to sign the manifesto. She made a big fuss about it. In order to make herself capable of saying no, she was indeed obliged to create a work of memoir. Page after page, she recalls the humiliations and exclusions, of all these "daughters and sisters of educated men" who could not go to Cambridge like their brothers. She refuses to record the fact that this past is bygone. She certainly celebrates the "sacred year," 1919, when, in England, women with diplomas gained the right to exercise certain liberal professions, but she cites at leisure the feeble snickering, the vulgar and violent opposition of those who were nevertheless attentive fathers and

2. Also in the same manifesto "Not in Our Names": "A look at the repressed memories of European colonization teaches us that this pattern is not new. European colonizers consistently legitimized their rule in the name of 'civilizing the colonies.' This 'civilizing mission' was fundamentally gendered: it was often presented in terms of 'protecting' women from their 'oppressive cultures and men.' Back in their 'motherlands' however, these same colonizers were often found among the most vehement opponents to the women's struggles of the first feminist wave."

beloved brothers. To think that today those same men could ask their sisters to protect cultural and intellectual freedom! "Suppose that the Duke of Devonshire, in his star and garter, stepped down into the kitchen and said to the maid who was peeling potatoes, with a smudge on her cheek: 'Stop your potato peeling, Mary, and help me to construe this rather difficult passage in Pindar,' would not Mary be surprised and run screaming to Louisa, the cook, 'Lawks, Louie, Master must be mad!'"[3]

But *Three Guineas* goes much further. Woolf doesn't stop with the incongruity of the Duke asking the kitchen girl to help him translate Pindar. She also wonders if it is good for this girl to climb up to the next floor. It is at this moment that the second letter to which she responds intervenes. This one comes from the female treasurer of an association seeking to help the daughters of educated men who are looking for employment in the profession which their education opened to them. In her answer, Woolf evokes the grand procession of men whom these girls, finally educated, seek to join. Their brothers and fathers already march there in cadence; proud bearers of titles and badges that their education brought them, they "walked according to rule, by hook or by crook made enough to keep the family house, somewhere, roughly speaking, in the West End, supplied with beef and mutton for all, and with education for Arthur."[4] If it were not just Arthur's education that was guaranteed, but also his sister Elizabeth's, should Elizabeth join Arthur in the grand procession?

In other words, Woolf situates herself in a period of transition where the question can still be posed: "Do we want to join this procession? And furthermore, what conditions will we accept? Where will it lead us, this procession of educated men?" Confronted with a proposition which we instinctively think must be accepted—wasn't it what so many women had struggled for?—Woolf is going to ask women to hesitate and not rush into it too quickly. She is

3. Virginia Woolf, *Three Guineas, op. cit.*, p. 130.
4. *Ibid.*, p. 92.

25

going to ask them to think, as women have always known how to do, as they have never stopped doing. "But you will object, you have no time to think, you have your battles to fight [...]. That excuse shall not serve you, Madame. As you know from your own experience, and there are facts that prove it, the daughters of educated men have always done their thinking hand to mouth; not under green lamps at study tables in the cloisters of secluded colleges. They have thought while they stirred the pot, while they rocked the cradle [...]. Think we must. Let us think in offices, in omnibuses, while we are standing in the crowd, watching Coronations and Lord Mayor's Shows, let us think as we pass the Cenotaph; and in White Hall; in the galleries of the House of Commons; in the Law Courts; let us think at baptisms and marriages and funerals. Let us never cease from thinking—what is this 'civilization' in which we find ourselves?"[5]

What is this civilization where appeals are made to culture and intellectual freedom as if they could stop wars, but whose institutions responsible for cultivating and transmitting culture and free thought work as assembly lines producing beings that Woolf describes as both submissive and violent, thirsting, if not for money, then for recognition, ready for all sorts of brutality if they feel that the abstract ideals that give them their identity are threatened? What is this society "that sink[s] the private brother, whom many of us have reason to respect, and inflates in his stead a monstrous male, loud of voice, hard of fist, childishly intent upon scoring the floor of the earth with chalk marks, within whose mystic boundaries human beings are penned, rigidly, separately, artificially[?]"[6] *Think we must.*

---

5. *Ibid.*, p. 94-95.

6. *Ibid.*, p. 160.

3

CREATING A "WE"

In order to find the strength to write *Three Guineas*, Virginia Woolf had to create a "we," one that encompassed the "daughters and sisters of educated men." She created the idea of a sisterhood at a time when such women could only dream of going to the university or engaging in a profession with some access to culture (Woolf herself had to learn Greek at home with a private female tutor).

One could object that this "think we must" of Virginia Woolf is an elitist proposition, addressed, as it was, only to the daughters and sisters of wealthy educated men. But we have experienced this in a different mode: in a way that makes it inseparable from the creation of a memory that may be a source of resistance. For Woolf it was not a question of affirming membership in a social class for which education should have been a right, unjustly withheld from girls. It was a question of situating herself, actively: not as a "woman" who finds herself part of a family that had the means to give her a private education, at home, but as the descendant of all those women of whom nothing more was expected other than what was demanded of a housewife, wife and mother, and who, dully, obstinately, braving ridicule and in a perfectly disinterested manner since they could not nourish any hope of a career or public recognition, resisted the sugar-coated objection of their father, "but my darling, you lack nothing...." These are women who sought to create and to live by all available means. To call oneself a daughter of these mothers, or of these aunts who remained old maids, is to fabricate for oneself an "ancestral memory," which could be called a fantasy, but from which Woolf demands the strength to resist, to not cede to the consensus—"let us forget the past, all together let us prevent the war."

The "we" created by Woolf in order to be able to say "not in our name" no longer includes us, who entered the university as if it was normal, however, as if that were expected. If something should concern us, wouldn't it instead be all those women and, to top it off, all those men for whom the University remains forbidden ground or a trap-filled terrain? And beyond that, of course, all those young girls excluded from education by traditions but most of all by poverty? However, what we have encountered in reading *Three Guineas* is the refusal of amnesiac mobilization. If Virginia Woolf speaks to us today, if she can help us to stand up to the test of orienting ourselves, it will not be in defense of a university subjugated to the market, forced to betray its democratic vocation. They will not make us forget that this university has failed to be transformed by the new arrivals who ventured to enter here.

We are indebted to Maria Puig de la Bellacasa[1] for this way of taking up the baton. *Think we must* designated, for her, those women who worked at the university with the intention of transforming it. Unlike us, they did not enter the university as amnesiacs, but with the question of what it meant, for them, to enter "as women." This heartfelt cry places in Woolf's lineage the women thinkers who, principally in the United States and Great Britain, have refused to accept, with gratitude or without

1. See Maria Puig de la Bellacasa. *Penser nous devons. Politiques féministes et construction des saviors* (Paris: L'Harmattan, 2013).

28

even thinking about it, the access finally granted to them by institutions of knowledge. Not that they would have refused admittance, as Woolf recommended, but they actively set about to explain their diagnosis of these places that from now on have officially been neutered. They refused to separate their pursuit of knowledge from the question of *who* produces this knowledge and *how* it is produced. They interrogated what is presented in science as neutral, objective. They asked the question, as feminists, of this science which presents itself as an "unmarked" category. They dared to re-mark what the scientists' claim to universality makes invisible. "There! There can be no doubt of the odor now. The cat is out of the bag; and it is a Tom."[2]

Unlike those woman thinkers (feminists, postfeminists, or *queer*, all denominations signaling important differences, but that Maria Puig has nevertheless chosen to place within the continuity of the collective adventure that interests her), Woolf was not familiar with the distinction between biological sex and the socio-historical construction of gender. But she had no need for that because, for her, the daughters and sisters of those men who were benefitting from a university education had no privilege with regard to thought and intellectual freedom other than perhaps the fact of having endured exclusion from the procession and therefore having been forced to cultivate the four virtues without which, according to Woolf, there is no intellectual freedom: preferring ridicule or derision to celebrity and praise; practicing chastity, that is to say, refusing to prostitute one's brain; contenting oneself with poverty, earning just enough money to live adequately and not a cent more; and keeping one's freedom from artificial loyalties, those that enlist, mobilize, and make one howl with the wolves. "They [the daughters of educated men] are immune, through no merit of their own, from certain compulsions. To protect culture and

2. Virginia Woolf, *Three Guineas*, op.cit, p. 78.

29

intellectual freedom in practice would mean, as we have said, ridicule and chastity, loss of publicity and poverty. But those, as we have seen, are their familiar teachers."[3] And it is in order to defend those virtues that Woolf, in her response to the third letter, imagines a "society of marginals," deliberately abandoning any situation that involved "making oneself known," refusing all stakes that encourage the prostitution of thought and the brutality of the ensuing relationships.

Who knows: perhaps this society exists as a network of complicity among those women who may have chosen an imperceptible future? But we are not among them—or if we are, it is only in a mode that must not be put on display, a mode which concerns no one. And today the feminist thinkers at the universities whom Maria addressed are no different. They publish, write their curriculum vitae, apply for positions, urge their female students to do the same, and there is no reason to reproach them for this—it must be like this or feminism (and post-feminism, etc.) will not be able to exist at the university. Quite simply, this is the price that must be paid.

To put the epistemological and conceptual debates that shook up *gender studies* with regard to the feminist politics of knowledge, as Maria does, under the sign of Virginia Woolf's "Think we must," was not meant to describe the actual state of affairs. It is unclear whether one can still find the disinterested culture in a university milieu, indifferent to the effects of branding, or the ridicule of a process that does not conform to the definition of the stakes that count. Like the "we" of the sisters and daughters of educated men, the "we" of university feminists has been created to incite thought, that is to say: to resist. For Maria Puig it was a question of resuscitating the active memories of this resistance of feminists who have struggled for a transformation of the university that Virginia had not thought possible—the

3. *Ibid.*, p. 152.

university as a place where one would think! But, as part of the "not in our name" movement, she also meant to celebrate an event that marked the history of American feminism: the "fussing intrusion" toward the middle of the 1980s, of those women who could not and would not recognize themselves in the manner in which white sisters spoke "in the name of women," notably forgetting that if their grandmothers had been subjugated, assigned to a role of wife and mother, they had also had Black slaves, subjugated to them. Or if they denounced the non-sharing of domestic tasks, free labor, most of them benefitted from the services of housekeepers, who were most often women of color. The women of color's challenge may well recall Woolf's refusal of mobilization for the values of the civilization that were proposed to her. And the acceptance of this challenge to *think*, even if uncomfortable or painful, enriched American feminism.

4

AS WOMEN?

Those first daughters of Virginia seem distant to us, since, in the universities of our regions, the idea that academic knowledge has an odor, and that odor is that of a "Tom," of a male, makes us snicker. Wouldn't practicing a science "as women" assume that a Galileo in lace clothing would have characterized falling bodies in some other way? That a Newton in a skirt would have produced a different celestial mechanics? The French (and Belgian) universities have kept the banner of a neutral and universal science flying high—have proudly maintained that the question of who practices science and to whom it is taught is henceforth only a matter of equal opportunity. And this banner is not only one that forbids asking the question of what is required by the presence of newly arrived students in a university labeled "democratic," today it is equally brandished by too many "republican" feminists in opposition to girls who do not graciously accept the equation "emancipated = unveiled."

Because few echoes—perhaps only deformed, snickering, accusatory echoes—reach us about what the American feminist philosopher Sandra Harding has called the "science question in feminism," we are going to dwell for a moment on this adventure at a time when women endeavored, in the heart of academic research, to make a difference that mattered.

From the point of view of feminists who have adopted the notion of gender, it goes without saying that science presents itself as neutral. For gender designates not only a socio-historical construction, but an asymmetrical one at that. There is an "unmarked" gender, which is presented as "normal" and in sharp contrast with the one defined as "the marked gender." The difference between marked and unmarked is found each time that a category is "invisible;" what it designates becomes then synonymous with a standard permitting the characterization of what "marks" those males and females who stray from the norm. Thus the category "man" is considered a universal, and the fact that it designates only 45% of humanity is made invisible. But one standard can hide another. That's what feminists discovered when "women of color" questioned their "white" sisters and contested the manner in which they represented, in both senses of the term, the "woman gender." White women had to accept that "white" was also an "unmarked" category, and that their analysis of gender relations situated them as "white women."

If there is a type of "unmarked" category, it is that of so-called academic practices—in particular, scientific practice. Before this question became the object of critical attention for feminists, science was considered to be the work of "humans," for a long time exclusively that of men, though only for reasons of socio-historical contingency. It was understood that this science would not change if women took their rightful place in the collective effort. In other words, women were welcome in science on the condition that they did not make themselves noticed as women, that they presented themselves as "unmarked" scientists among the others.

But the case of science also demonstrates the risks of the choice presented to those women who are both feminists and scientists. Let us hasten to note that we, as (Belgian) philosophers, do not run any such risks. Not that philosophy does not make claims to universality, but today these claims are in no way taken seriously—notably by scientists—to such a degree that philosophy itself constitutes a "marked" category. "Ah, philosophers!" can occasionally be said in the same tone as "Ah, women!" In contrast, if one could speak of the "science question in feminism," it's because within feminism the matter was considered a true question, even a dilemma.

From this point of view, the history of primatology is particularly interesting to us, insofar as women have explored and displayed the possibility of a relation, to be claimed or not, between different ways of doing science and the question of gender. They have measured the risks, they have hesitated and they have continued to do it.

It must be said that the situation was quite exceptional. At the end of the 1960s and the beginning of the 1970s, the first women primatologists returned from fieldwork involving primates with observations that were quite different than the narratives that had been imposed up to then. The data from our fieldwork, these primatologists claimed, do not permit us to support the contention that females have the very limited social role that had been attributed to them in prior studies. As for the universality, almost uncontested until then, of a highly hierarchical organization among members of a group, it was submitted to the most severe criticism: the intense competition and incessant conflicts over resources, food, lodging sites and females which had been observed would now be seen either as the result of superficial or biased observations or linked to the research conditions. "Hierarchy is a myth", and "dominance is an artifact of research," affirmed Shirley Strum and Thelma Rowell, respectively.

That these new observations have been largely due to women scientists has obviously given rise to the hypothesis—and its corollary propositions—that women scientists would observe differently than men. Concretely, women's research would be more closely associated with the individuality of the observed apes; women would stay longer in the field, which permitted them to practice the method of habituation and observe other things; women would pay more attention to the context; women would try to be attentive to the questions that those whom they were observing posed, rather than imposing their own questions; they would be more attentive to females....[1]

However, this proposition has divided women primatologists, and we would like to make the voice of those who refuse the hypothesis heard in order to show the dilemma that they had to resolve. Their choice has sometimes been characterized as an adhesion to an "empiricist" conception of science. Claiming only "good facts," producers of a better science, they would subscribe to the consensual perspective of an "unmarked" scientific progress. But for them the question did not reside there.[2]

1. In the summary of reports that Haraway gives (Donna Haraway, *Primate Visions, Gender, Race, and Nature in the World of Modern Science*, New York and London: Routledge, 1989, p. 397, note 13) one will find mentioned: the renouncing of control, the will to be connected to the problem of the one being interrogated rather than to a theory that determines the answers, characteristics that are subordinated to a high tendency toward skepticism in regard to generalizations, a clear preference for more conceptualized explanations, impregnated with specificity, diversity, complexity. According to the feminist primatologist Linda Fedigan, "the values traditionally defined as feminine may lead women to generally be more persistent and patient, willing to wait for the material to speak for itself rather than forcing answers out of it, and envisioning themselves as more connected to the subject matter than in control of it," cited by Linda Schiebinger, *Has Feminism Changed Science?* (Cambridge: Harvard University Press, 1999), p. 6.

2. See Shirley Strum, Linda Fedigan (eds.), *Primate Encounters: Models of Science, Gender and Society*, (Chicago: University of Chicago Press, 2000). This important book comes out of a conference organized by Fedigan and Strum which brought together primatologists, feminist thinkers and specialists from *Science Studies*. This conference, a rare occurrence in the history of the sciences, associated primatologists and those researchers who have taken their practice as an argument, and in doing so tried to go beyond the stage of quarreling. And if that was the "difference?" Even if Fedigan and Strum have asserted their strong reticence to the idea of a stable difference between practices according to the gender of the primatologists, they have refused "trench warfare," at a time when a rather virile and stupid confrontation has mobilized the defenders of scientific reason against its critics (the so-called "science wars").

Accepting the compliment of having practiced science in another way—especially once the discoveries had been recognized as incontestable—and of having done this as women, put some of them in the position of being in contradiction with the very motive that had guided their practice: they had worked as they did because their apes demanded it of them in order to be well-studied. It was not due to being women, but due to the apes that they learned to pose more relevant questions. Admittedly, they affirmed, they focused all their attention to the individuality of the males and females they were observing, they devoted a long time to being present beside them[3] and they gave back to the females a place that had been denied to them in social interactions. But these differences were not attributable to the fact that they were women scientists. It was a question of the exigencies of the profession. One cannot, one should not, do otherwise when seeking to describe beings so personal and singular, experienced beings with a long and complicated life, with differentiated roles that matter to the group, a group whose functioning is too

---

3. The difference of the duration of fieldwork was aligned with gender (several months on the average for men, several years for women). This difference may in fact be explained by the (very great) difficulty for women primatologists, in the 1960s, to obtain academic positions: thus they stayed with their apes rather than seeking, in vain, to make an academic career. The question of the duration, and consequently of habituation, would arise more from a condition of inequality than of difference—even if, of course, one is still free to ask if the latter is not in play in the acceptance of a highly taxing commitment without promise of recognition by "one's peers." In any case, the answer cannot be general. Attention must be paid to the historical, political and material contexts and conditions in which this duration is inscribed or modified. Thus, the fact that Japanese male primatologists have also privileged long durations indicates appreciably different conditions. It is by forgetting this type of attention that one comes to question the strange similarity between the practice of women primatologists and that of Japanese researchers (habituation, and thus proximity, as a condition of the practice, individual recognition, interest in the role of females and in the innovative capabilities of the apes). Strum and Fedigan (*Primate Encounters, op. cit.*) demonstrate, as Haraway had already done, the way in which narrative reconstructions of the fieldwork harken back to what anthropologists call orientalism, an exoticization of practices such that of women and of Japanese researchers, tending to characterize them as "other" because of differences, more or less fantasized, with the dominant model.

sophisticated to be reduced to a few simple determinants.

The refusal of certain primatologists to define themselves "as women" is therefore not a question of prudence or empiricist prejudice. They are also engaged in a struggle. But they are struggling so that their profession may become worthy of what their area of study demands: a focus on the primates to whom they are indebted for having learned the interesting things that are now known because of their work. For them, this is what defines them as good scientists. If they accepted that their animals were interesting because they were studied by women, they would nullify the very aim of their research: to show how interesting these animals are. They did not ask them women's questions (apes, then, would lose all interest), they tried to learn from them what the pertinent questions were. For each of these primatologists, what characterizes their practice is not that it is an "other" or "successor" practice, but one which they can honor as good scientific practice.

A striking similarity exists between this attitude of primatologists and the way in which the biologist Barbara McClintock described the course of her success, and notably her decision to no longer *use* corn to elucidate genetic enigmas, but to learn "with it," to understand its functioning, in the most intimate sense of the term, to interrogate it while accepting its own, exigent conditions. Admittedly, Barbara McClintock never had to hesitate about presenting her science as another, feminine, kind of science—it was not yet the time—but she made it clear that the way she learned with the corn was good scientific practice, not an alternative to the reductive violence associated with "male science."[4]

When Shirley Strum made her choice—primates matter, and the way they matter would be weakened by insisting on the fact that it is "as a woman" that she characterizes them—she was thinking of a question

---

4. See Evelyn Fox Keller, *A Feeling for the Organism: The Life and Work of Barbara McClintock* (New York: Freeman, 1983).

that McClintock's corn did not call for, namely the threats that men pose to them. But, like McClintock, she also says that being a good scientist cannot be summed up as collecting good facts or better facts, but requires learning how to address those that are being interrogated. Whether it concerns primates or corn, these beings matter for those women who are addressing them, and because they matter, a true dilemma exists. Should one choose the "proper manner" to address them in the context of an internal struggle waged within the sciences, or should one create an example of another way to practice science, "as women?" There is a conflict of loyalty, and taking a position here corresponds to a strategic choice. For a scientist, to claim that it is "as a woman" that she signals the singularity of her practice is certainly a way to contribute to the feminist struggle, but at the price of giving ammunition to those who were precisely waiting for it in order to avoid questions which demand hesitation, lucidity, and attention to problems of pertinence. The woman who is a bother will no longer be a colleague but a distraction who intends to "politicize science," to make it serve a cause that is "unscientific." What is it then that matters the most: fighting for a science attentive to pertinence or confirming the hypothesis that science as a gendered practice is incapable of such attention?

The manner in which the work of Adrienne Zihlman has been greeted reveals the brutality of the rejection to which the female researcher is exposed when she presents herself as a feminist. The hypothesis of the "woman gatherer" that she theorizes and documents responds to the widely accepted—and rather virile—hypothesis of the "man hunter," assumed to realize the process of hominization. This hypothesis implies accepting the causal role of women in this process, taking into consideration that the reaper-gatherer also required tools, which constituted an innovation that participated in the evolution of the ways of being human.

It is important to emphasize that Zihlman did not exclude the theory of man the hunter but multiplied the possible narrative models. She wanted to enrich history, by multiplying the causes, inventions, and events; what has prevailed is the idea that she intended to bring down the male from a decisive role. No hesitation was possible: the proposition of putting a pacific and cooperative female on center stage was "unscientific." Her thesis could appear all the more unscientific as it put cooperation, not bellicose competition, at the forefront. Yet "true science" is recognized by the way in which it destroys our illusions and makes us face truths that we must accept, despite our personal or political "preferences."

The rejection that Zihlman experienced has been even more brutal because the scientists clearly identified the theoretical proposition with the feminist commitment of its author. As Donna Haraway stresses, this story constitutes a veritable allegory of the relations between a marked gender and sex, and the unmarked gender and sex of science. "Zihlman's science cannot be allowed to coexist with her feminism, which has turned an already marked gender into politics, which is quintessentially the marked "other" to unmarked science [...]. The narratives of hominization are inextricably entwined to the narratives of citizenship, rationality and gender."[5] This is different from McClintock's corn, where the eventuality of a feminine style of scientific practice posed only "epistemological" or general questions, with contrasts such as "holistic" or "analytic" approaches. The singularity of primatology is its proximity to the question of the difference between "man" and "animal," a question that fascinates scientists as well as religious scholars and most philosophers. And Zihlman crossed the line, for her proposition demonstrated the political dimension of the supposedly unmarked scientific version of her colleagues. If it is hunting, and soon afterwards, war, that forged the difference between man and animal,

5. Donna Haraway, *Primate Visions, op. cit.,* p. 346.

aren't these the impassable horizons of all communal life? Zihlman "polluted" science at the very point when it was proclaiming its role as the giver of lessons, recalling the objectivity of facts to idealistic people who delight in illusions. She thus brings to the power of allegory the question posed to feminist and scientific women: claiming to do science "as women" is to win an already prepared medal as a martyr, but it is also to see the science for which one struggles identified as a pollution of science.

5

TAKING UP THE BATON?

There are stories that need to be ceaselessly reactivated in order to be relayed with new givens and new unknowns. It was necessary to reactivate the history of women who posed the question of a "different" science in order to affirm that this was not an "epistemological dream," that they had to confront a true dilemma. Contesting the way that science defines itself, including the completely political requirement of separating science from politics, was to risk being retorted, whatever one proposes, that it is not science; in other words, offering ready-made arguments to those who will exclude the questions. Not doing this is not a simple cautionary measure; it is a choice, and a costly one at that. In order to change a science, in order to steer it toward addressing its objects in another way, one must behave in a way that will avoid inciting accusations from colleagues, and thus ratify the opposition between science and opinion. Relaying includes knowing that being true to the question one relays, requires its transformation.

It is not a question of discussing the reasons why Virginia Woolf's pessimism has been verified. Certainly, the university which today claims to be "democratized," which claims to be open to everybody (as long as not too

43

much attention is given to proportions), no longer has much in common with the "sacred" places, upon whose thresholds the sisters of Woolf stood. But the university also has little in common with the vibrant, thinking place envisioned by American feminists (and those of Northern Europe). These women in struggle are still alive, but most often they are segregated in the fields that Americans call *studies* (*gender, queer, cultural, post-colonial* or *critical studies*). One can surely deplore the absence or the great weakness of such studies in our French-speaking countries, but it is necessary to recognize that their professionalization elsewhere is not at all what had been sought.

Times have changed. The question of a science capable of opening itself to questions that it has traditionally judged "non-scientific"—including the questions raised by the definition and the requirements of a scientific career and by the formation of future scientists—belongs more than ever to the future. But such a future, if it is to ever become present, will probably never come from a dynamic generated inside the university—who knows, perhaps it will come from outside, from those men and women who will learn to become actively concerned by those questions that they are not supposed to meddle with. In that case, the stakes would change once again—Zihlman's descendants would have their chance, because instead of warding off the specter of "opinion," against which "science" must be defended, scientists would have to address active, knowledgeable, demanding communities.

However, today, such a change is merely speculation. If the odor of science has changed, it is because components of fear and frustration have been added. And we must not fool ourselves; this is nothing to be happy about. If Woolf could evoke the brutality of brothers preparing to join their fathers in the grand procession of educated men, one may fear that their descendants today, humiliated, degraded, managed in the way that the private sector has learned to "manage human resources," have only become more ferocious. For let us not be fooled, the mystic boundaries noted by Woolf will survive to the extent that such boundaries do not have the purpose of protecting an interior worthy of existence, but of marking what must be excluded. Scientists, if they had been confident and assured of the meaning and value of what they do, could have, perhaps, taken an interest in what called them into question. Those scientists who today know that they depend on partners in the private sector defend the opposition of science/opinion all the more fiercely. In our current times, at the slightest suspicion of "relativism," there is a closing of the ranks— there is no discussion, one simply takes up arms against the irrational threat.

We are philosophers. We have not had to make the choices which feminist scientists or even those supporting them have been confronted with, because the accusation of "that is not philosophy" does not at all have the same exclusionary weight as "that is not science." Or, more precisely, it is merely one reason for exclusion among many others: merely a part of the philosophers' routine of judging that most of their colleagues are not "true" philosophers. Admittedly, as we have already noted, our research could incite suspicion or disdain from certain colleagues, but we cannot and do not want to adorn ourselves with the honors of those women and men who would have faced the choice defined by Virginia Woolf: conform or live on the margins. For us, philosophy was liable to be what we were doing, and we have not felt the slightest heroism in living that possibility.

But such a possibility is condemned by the new mystic boundaries that are taking hold—true philosophy being now defined by the problematics admissible in the top-rated journals. Of course, there are still interstices where one may breathe. GECo, for example, at the University of Brussels, where Maria Puig's questions have found resonance and consequences, where the question of what

Three Guineas makes us think today[1] was turned into a collective matter of concern. GECo is an interstitial place where one tries to create, to cultivate, to understand the meaning of, "thinking together"; where situations are tried whose success is to make one lose the taste for rhetorical dramatization and arguments of authority. But like all interstitial places, for GECo, "to resist is (just) to exist." For an interstitial place is not a place for heroic resistance. It only exists if it is capable of holding fast, of determining its own make-up, of fabricating its own *raison d'être*, that is, if what it does is also what keeps it alive.

It is thus necessary for us to resist the sugar-coated objection that would say to us "but don't you see, since a group of this kind exists, and since you two could freely choose your fields of research, the university remains a place of freedom." In these cases, it is a question of small, local successes, which in no way prevent the university from functioning as it functions. Quite the contrary, we could even serve as an example, demonstrating its great tolerance. You could almost say that we are a little like kept women who show off the generosity and wealth of the man who pays them.

But how do we take back up a collective adventure that is multiple and ceaselessly reinvented, not on an individual basis, but in a way that passes the baton, that is to say, affirms new givens and new unknowns? How do we reactivate Virginia's cry once again and make anew, "think we must," without riding on her coattails?

1. Three members of the GECo, Marion Jacot-Descombes, Nathalie Trussart and Benedikte Zirouni, first worked together, then organized a passing of the baton to the group as a whole, which, in turn, undertook the organization of a one-day workshop. "Thinking today, with Virginia Woolf's *Three Guineas*," was a question of bringing together those women and men for whom the situation of the university today was a concern. They were not looking for rhetorical generalities or mobilizing denunciations, but were open to the experience of "thinking together." Virginia Woolf was present through five brief presentations of fragments of her text with the worries but also the dreams and fabulations of those who chose the excerpts. The workshop was seeking, and we think succeeded in creating, a "moment of thought" that would not have incited Woolf's anger and distrust.

We have benefitted from a mere window of opportunity which made it possible for us to do our own thinking, and we will be able to continue to do so, no doubt, because we have secured academic positions, in the manner of aging witnesses, of what was possible.

Woolf had counseled her contemporaries to only go to the university to look for resources for a sober and independent life, from an intellectual and economic point of view. But reactivating her cry does not mean retroactively proving her right, that is to say discretely deserting, without fuss, the places from which we would have understood there was nothing more to expect. Deserting the "privileged" place that Woolf had denounced, so be it. But deserting a university that has been "democratized," that claims to bring together the children of Mary, the kitchen girl, with those of the Duke of Devonshire and also those of Abdallah, that's not the same thing. That would really resemble a refusal of the aristocratic type. If "think we must," this is the case at the university as well as everywhere else, for everywhere the question of "this civilization in which we find ourselves" is from now on quite openly asked.

And thus, if we must pass on the baton, the "we" of Woolf, we must dare "to make" the relay; that is to create, fabulate, in order not to despair. In order to induce a transformation, perhaps, but without the artificial loyalty that would assemble "in the name of a cause," no matter how noble it might be. We don't know if it is possible to save this wretched university whose passivity we understand better, thanks to Woolf. The "mystic boundaries," the abstract ideals may nourish some moaning, even individual resistances, but not the collective ability to do otherwise. We know that, if our world is ever to be saved, it would not be in the mystic terms of a crusade, of a re-conquest of past glories. In order to relay Woolf's cry, this "think we must" she addressed to the daughters of educated men, to those young women who knew how to think while stirring

47

pots and rocking cradles, we needed to first of all learn to make a formal record of what happened to us; that is, to hear it as an appeal not to begin anew but to begin again. Without a guarantee, without the slightest assurance that this might make a difference, that this might contribute to inciting possibilities to effectively resist. Thus knowing from the beginning that it's ridiculous or even derisory. Simply with the conviction that, in any case, everything begins this way, with experimentation ceaselessly recommencing, with the sense of the possible always being reborn.

Beginning again first of all means learning again to transform our relation to the current state of affairs and notably learning to try out the idea that we are a part of these "new arrivals" of whom it is said that their presence at the university was "normal," because it was required by democratic progress. This is somewhat counter-intuitive because we have never encountered any of the difficulties faced by the children of Mary or of Abdallah. Once again, we have nothing to complain about. It is not a question of complaining, or claiming one's place among the victims, but a question of experimentation. And, in this case, it was about trying out the effects of this hypothesis: the choices we have made as philosophers, the choices of our objects of research and how to treat them, we would have made as women or as women philosophers. We thus experimented with the idea that, if we had never been aware of philosophizing as women, it's because we had accepted our presence at the university as "normal." Because we had accepted that the vocation of thought transcends gender, and that, more than any other field, philosophy must manifest this vocation.

It is from this point of departure that it has been a question for us of "beginning again," starting from this somewhat fantastic hypothesis that, perhaps, our colleagues were not wrong to consider us suspicious, that perhaps we had really intruded where thought is defined as a man's affair.[2] We would not stop at the fact that the kind of thinking which each one of us has practiced in her own way, never directly concerned "marked" questions, those that one cannot pose without knowing that in so doing, one will pose them "as women"—the body, medicine, sensuality, experience of domination, sexual relations, etc. Certainly, such questions are not foreign to us; we are not extra-terrestrials. But what we wanted was to try out together, through a reciprocal catalysis, the effects which might be induced by this proposition: that thought, as we practiced it, we practiced "as women."

---

2. In fact, the somewhat anecdotal point of departure of our common cogitations has been the mischievous little pamphlet whose title announces its content, written by Frédéric Pagès, *Philosopher ou l' art de clouer le bec aux femmes* [To philosophize or the art of shutting women's mouths](Paris: Mille et une Nuits, 2006). Pagès emphasizes how few women philosophers have (in France) got high-level recognition. This, he maintains, is not a matter of chance, neglect, or even a simple delay, but rather one of a lack of affinity between philosophy as it is practiced and what makes women think and speak. Philosophy would have excluded from its own uses and field ways of feeling, being affected and speaking as an affected being—all ways that can be attached to the feminine. This, however, leaves open a question: are women specialists in these matters or have they grasped them like the left-overs of a banquet from which they were excluded? At this point our cogitations began.

6

THE PERSONAL IS POLITICAL

Even those women who are strangers to the feminist tradition are familiar with the famous formula of Simone de Beauvoir: "One is not born a woman, one becomes a woman." As philosophers, we have learned that this formula has as its vocation the de-essencing of what it means to be a woman. One "becomes" a woman, and the term "become" refers us back to a process already completed, a process that has modeled each child of the female sex into a woman, that is, into a product of particular social and historical conditions which forge roles, ways of thinking, attitudes as a function of sexual membership (what is now called "gender"). There was thus nothing to learn, only to unlearn: it is because women have been modeled as women that they think like women. Our path is the inverse. It has not been a question for us of a retrospective elucidation (we would have thought like women, even if we didn't know it), and even less of an emancipatory enterprise, aiming to break the model. It has been a question of both of us engaging together in trying out a "becoming woman," in the sense of a transformation in the present.

Experimentation is not decided in the mode of a lucidity weighing reasons and consequences. Reasons and consequences come after. Our moment of decision did bear on or belong to the experience of sharing new thoughts, new laughs, new imaginations. It was the decision to not let this experience dissolve into the passive tissue of the "lived," but to seek to make something out of it. That is why we think that Woolf's cry, think we must, of which we are experimenting with the possibility of our relaying, has the efficacy of an induction. The cry induces an experience that carries with it the question of taking up the baton, of attempting this experiment.

The first effective aspect of the induction is to enable us able to respond to the question "who are the we who must think?": we are among those women who have been where Woolf said we must not go, or in any case not stay, for staying there, seeking to make a career in the university, is to be captured by it (for both young men and women). And this efficacy does not involve mournful lucidity; rather it implies creation—creation of a transformation of the relation to memory, a creation that is produced by every work of memoir. Situated by this "we," of the "unfaithful daughters of Virginia Woolf," the evocation of our experiences becomes anonymous, speaking of something other than us—as are anonymous the inflexion points of a life, those encounters or decisions, of which one is never the author even though, whether one knows it or not, one never ceases exploring their consequences or trying to make sense of them; as became anonymous the anecdotes exchanged by those women who were becoming feminists, during encounters where, each one in her own way, and each one with all the others, made real what they had lived on the personal level which was (also) political.

That the personal might be political should never be stated as a generality. For it is not a question of a complaint, but rather of a re-appropriation of the past, like an after-shock that makes possible active experimentation as well as fabulation. Generalities don't lead to much, mostly to feelings of powerlessness and resentment. Actively orienting ourselves within a fabulatory mode brings to light resources that make it possible to not tumble down that slope of powerless complaint. Such are the resources that Woolf produced by summoning the ancestral memory of those ridiculous women who persisted in sticking to a course which could not lead anywhere. And it is these resources that we must produce once again, grounded in the present, in order to take up the baton. Finally, again and always, we must think about "this civilization in which we find ourselves," and which, in this case, made us think that going to the university is "normal."

The induction passes through us but, of course, it does not stop with us. We will soon experiment with the possibility of endowing Woolf's cry with the power to produce and induce participation in the relay. Would other women who have also committed themselves to those university careers, from which Woolf said we must flee, accept joining it and assure the passing of the baton? We had to test what Woolf's cry might induce and produce for these women.

But, it must be said, these others were already present, virtually, from the time when it was no longer a question of speaking of a personal "we," each of us recalling how we had found a way to do this or that, how to refuse this or that, to fabricate for herself such and such a persona. For Woolf's cry bars the possibility of envisioning ourselves in any way as having been particularly courageous or original. In a way, what we experienced is rather similar to what happened in those meetings where women becoming feminists explored together what it meant to think that "the personal is political." Convoking and evoking personal memories had as its first effect the transformation of what had been up to then lived as empirical, unattached, and anecdotal into a mode where bits of history made sense to others, became detached from psychological and intimate reasons with which each woman had until then associated them. Speaking about our different ways of doing things, of our refusals, but also of those feelings of having been displaced, of the feelings of discomfort that cropped up at every turn, was no longer a matter of chatter but of commonality: of becoming capable of feeling and saying together: "This matters." To be able to make a joyful fuss about it.

In this sense, accepting the "think we must" had a triple effect, in the same way that the word "*reconnaissance*" has a triple meaning. Taking up the baton of Woolf's cry means first of all accepting with gratitude that something has been given to us, a something which modifies the relationship that each one of us maintains with what she had done up to then. We were no longer two singularities, but particular cases of a fabulated "we." And it is as such that we could get to know each other again, get to re-know each other as relays among others. But, to become receptive to the power of Woolf's cry, it was necessary to finally, fabulously, and retroactively recognize what had made each of us think. To know again is to *re-suscitate*,[1] [*re-susciter*] that is, to once again take up a story, our own, but in a different mode, as if each time it added new dimensions to a question that up to then we had not posed, or had posed differently.

This "we," questioning how what had provided resources for one of us could do so for the other, did not of course erase the differences in our two journeys. Our matters of interest are different, our ages as well: one was already working as a philosopher when the other started her studies. Our encounter itself could translate this inequality: one, having read the books of the other, sent her very first manuscript to her, asking for advice. Producing, one for the other, the resource that granted

---

1. Once again, we are indebted to Maria Puig for learning of the contrast between resuscitate (from resurrection) and re-suscitate, a contrast that on the one hand insists upon the creative dimension of taking up a problem again, a creative dimension that modifies it by the very gestures that assure relaying it, and on the other hand, by the fact that this creation cannot be disassociated from the question posed by taking it up again.

us the possibility of reciprocal recognition, has created between us the kind of equality which permitted us to think that we could write together.

Initially, what we knew is that neither one of us had embraced, as a vocation, this exercise of thought that is called philosophy. Not that we were wondering if we would be capable of it, if our names would be worthy to one day be added to those of the authors whose texts we were reading, or would be included in the dictionaries of philosophy (they have not been …). If we had doubts, they suggested rather a certain analogy with the "I would prefer not to" of the clerk Bartleby, that living enigma in Melville's short story who, obstinately and with no other explanation except this formula, refuses to be engaged, to fill any one of the functions that his "boss" proposes, a boss becoming more and more obsessed, fascinated, ready to give anything to him if only he would accept it. Except, of course, that we are not living enigmas, that we have not driven any of our bosses crazy, that both of us have done what had to be done to earn our diplomas and even to launch our "careers" (which means beginning to work on our doctoral dissertations). Simply, if doing philosophy meant seriously considering inescapable dilemmas, irresolvable alternatives, injunctions that put us up against a wall, we would prefer not to. And when we saw the authors that we were reading striking a heroic pose, as if the destiny of humanity or the vocation of the subject was in play in the question they were posing, it must be said that we were laughing up our sleeves, knowing full well that this laugh could mean that we would never be "real" philosophers.

But the principal difference with Bartleby, a masculine figure, unfathomable and fascinating, invented by a man, is that, at the end of the short story, he dies (in prison for loitering, preferring not to eat), whereas we are living. Moreover each of us has found her personal way to inscribe herself in this somewhat bizarre story that is called philosophy.

And it is there that the political did play itself out for us from what each one of us has lived as "personal," as the way that each of us had earned the right to "do philosophy," no matter what our colleagues thought of it. It is there that the "you too!" signaling the transmutation of the personal into the political began, and then retroactively took on importance, though at first it might seem anecdotal.

It was no longer a question of a refusal, of an embarrassment, of an "I would prefer not to," but rather a trust in the possibility that a problem, once freed from the generalities that take it hostage, once it is given a chance, might spread out to unexpected dimensions, becoming something that obliged one to think, that is, something that makes one go from refusal to creation. If there was a "we" susceptible of answering, retroactively, Woolf's cry, think we must, it was the one who discovered itself capable of making a whole big fuss about what could be reduced to a mere fact: we had, each one of us on her own behalf, made use of the same fable, that of the twelfth camel.[2]

The fable of the twelfth camel tells the story of an old Bedouin who, sensing that his end was near, called his three sons to him in order to divide his goods among them. He said to them: *My sons, I bequeath half of my goods to the eldest, a quarter to the second, and you, my last one, I give you one-sixth*. At the death of their father, the sons were very perplexed for the goods of the father were nothing more than eleven camels. How could they be divided? War between the brothers seemed inevitable. Seeing no solution, they went to the neighboring village to seek the advice of an old wise man. He reflected, then shook his head: *I cannot solve this problem. All I can do for you is to give you my only camel. He is old, he is skinny and no longer very robust, but perhaps he will help you*. The sons brought

2. Vinciane Despret, *Ces émotions qui nous fabriquent* (Paris: Les Empêcheurs de penser en rond, 1999). Isabelle Stengers. *Thinking with Whitehead* (Cambridge, Mass.: Harvard University Press, 2011) Originally published in French (Paris: Le Seuil, 2002).

the old camel back to the other camels and they divided them up: the first thus received six camels, the second three and the last two. That left the old weak camel that they were able to return to its owner.

With the twelfth camel, we could re-weave a motif that had been common to us and which came to be re-suscitated as such, as a retroactive and fabulatory effect of induction. It is not at all accidental that this fable came back to us when we tried to construct the "us" from "what happened to us." Its story is the story of "trusting a particular situation," a situation which appeared destined to lead to war. The sons were not confined "to preferring not" to make war, but, in consulting the old wise man, they took the chance that perhaps the problem might not lead to war. They gave its chance to a possible peace and the twelfth camel reconfigured the problem by revealing the unknown that the formulation of the problem concealed. Sharing an inheritance according to predetermined proportions requires that the sum of the apportioned parts be equal to the inheritance. But this does not prescribe what the calculation of the proportions must be based on.

Retroactively, we realize that the twelfth camel communicates for each one of us with a way to resist and create. To both of us the question was posed of "how to inherit" a practice, philosophy, defined most often by what Virginia Woolf would call "mystic boundaries," great problems that demand mobilization—ah! dissertation exercises where unhappy young people must decide Man's responsibility or his submission to some determinism or maybe his difference from Animals (when it was not from Women, several decades ago). We realize that we were able to share the inheritance of this field, long reserved for men in the name of a Reason which women would not be capable of, only to the extent that the field was in fact unable to prescribe the way it was to be inherited. That is, perhaps, how we would have thought "as women?"

Before giving space to other women's voices, we would like to present this first version of a "personal" that is learning to call itself "political"—an active refusal of a "genre" (gender) of thinking that was perhaps not wrong to mistrust women, these traitors, incapable of taking seriously the great problems that transform thought into a battlefield.

7

THE QUESTION OF INHERITANCE

The twelfth camel is not the solution to our question, no more than it was for the sons of the old Bedouin. Or, rather, it only became one for the sons because they had not only inherited eleven camels but, in going to consult the wise man, had made themselves heirs to a problem and defined the inheritance starting from this problem. Isn't that the very gesture that we have used in the preceding pages? We inherited a question of how to orient ourselves "as women," but it was in defining the inheritance starting from the question that it poses, the very question of taking it up again, that we could begin to construct a way of responding.

For Vinciane, the twelfth camel imposed itself when she was writing her PhD dissertation, where she was exploring the teachings that our tradition elaborated about emotions. How do we address these conflicting teachings, these confrontations between the question of knowing if emotions are biological or psychological, social or individual, natural and universal or local and culturally constructed, in the body, in the soul, or in the world? How do we receive each one of these theories or propositions formulated on the subject's emotional experience when each one defines itself precisely as incompatible with the others, as the possessor of the true explanation, exclusive of any other? It was not possible to take on the posture of a judge who would have sorted the theories according to a series of criteria, to each one its due, or the posture of a notary—to each one would be devolved its part of the truth: no more than the eleven camels, this type of inheritance does not allow itself to be divided up. How do we also avoid, the critical distance, the solution that the sons could have adopted if they had just accepted the situation as it presented itself: their father was just delirious? In Vinciane's case it would have meant turning one's back to the battle, following the controversies with the called-for indifference, and obtaining the prized academic title. Except that in the same way the sons' indifference would have been feigned, these theories cannot leave us indifferent. They do not limit themselves to describing or revealing what emotions are; they affect and nourish the way we are able to experience emotion. They involve our experiences and whether we want to or not, we inherit from such theories. It was a question of receiving, of inheriting, but at the same time resisting the threatening choice between accepting or declining, that is, constructing a situation which would be neither one of (feigned) indifference nor one of "speaking truth" about the emotion to which each one of these theories lay claim.

Women ethno-psychologists[1] have offered Vinciane the twelfth camel, permitting her to add a dimension to the problem which, retroactively, was missing. Admittedly, these ethno-psychologists were proposing a certain conception of emotions, a conception which affirms that one will not be moved in the same way if one is

1. In particular it was Catherine Lutz and Lila Abu Lughod, who were the two ethno-psychologists who helped her. See Catherine Lutz, *Unnatural Emotions: Everyday Sentiments on a Micronesian Atoll and Their Challenge to Western Theory* (Chicago: Chicago University Press, 1988) and Lila Abu Lughod, *Veiled Sentiments: Honor and Poetry in a Bedouin Society* (Berkeley: University of California Press, 1986), as well as their respective contributions to the book they have co-edited, *Language and the Politics of Emotions* (Cambridge: Cambridge University Press, 1990).

an Ifaluk of the western Pacific or a Bedouin Awlad 'Ali of the Egyptian desert. A cultural conception, therefore, able to contest other theories in their field. Except that the understanding that they proposed was not authorizing any form of exclusion of the other theories, quite the contrary. They articulated them by making perceptible the fact that these theories of emotions nourished our experience, these theories made us. Our emotions are biological because we cultivate them as such; they are locally universal; they pose the question of their authenticity because it is as such that we construct our experience of them. These ethno-psychologists were adding the singularity of our inheritance to the problem: the fact that emotions had been enlisted in our world as crucial stakes, sometimes concerning the organization of power relations (notably between men and women, women being considered in most of the theories as more emotional), sometimes the disciplinary fields (biology and psychology, for example); sometimes again in the separation of private and public spheres; sometimes finally in the moral and political question of autonomy, of will, of mastery of oneself, to cite only some of the domains where emotions play a major role for us.

To situate ourselves within the heart of our inheritance, as the ethno-psychologists were inviting us to do, is to understand the mutually exclusive characteristics of the roles associated with emotion differently. All the theoreticians of emotions share the ambition of speaking "truth," of extricating the authentic meaning of emotions; this is why finding one theory to be right means finding another to be wrong. For Vinciane, they all concerned a particular figure of translation, the school exercise called "theme" in French, when you have to translate a text from your own language into a foreign one. The basic value of the exercise is fidelity, conformity with the original text; this text has the power to designate the "good translation" since different translators know well what this wording, produced in their own language, "means." Each theory is in some way a "theme," claiming to constitute "the" translation faithful to the truth of the emotion. But can one give up such a claim? School teaches us that there are students who get zeroes in "theme" but write "versions," translations into their own language, with great feeling. There is a false symmetry between the two translation exercises, for it is only in the version that one can experience the multiplicity of ways to translate, and the choice to be made. A choice, which is not arbitrary, which wants to be "faithful," but here fidelity is not a norm one obeys, it is a problem to which no one response corresponds. No one will say that the version is "relative" to the translators, at least in the sad sense of relativism. Quite the contrary, the text written in the original language, which is not the language of any of the translators, brings them all together, presents them all with a problem which obliges them to activate the resources of their own language.

The twelfth camel transformed themes which were trying to translate what emotion "really is" into versions. Our inheritance makes emotion a problem, and it is this problem which brings together those who try to define how to speak truthfully about emotions. Everyone practices the art of the version, although perhaps some of these versions might have been richer if they were not dominated by the thematic ambition to silence others.

Passing from theme to version obviously does not resolve the problem, but it does transform it. The multiplicity of versions is no longer what must be overcome, or what one must acknowledge (a sad or ironic relativism). A version always signals the existence of other versions, versions which do not tell the same story, or offer variations; it keeps the memory of what it was up against, and against which it continues to develop. Its interest is not to erase all the others, but to create, or make apparent, relations which the others silenced, or to which they gave another meaning. A version is first of all a creative transformation, even if it is presented in the style of a theme and is proud of its fidelity to the original. And this transforms the position of the one who deals with the multiplicity of versions, because creation, far from being a weakness, explicitly affirms what the confrontation of rival themes implies: the importance, for all these versions, of the problem by which the versions multiply. Relativist irony would be to negate the implication; that is, to adopt a very strange position: showcasing the multiplicity of versions as "being relative," is also affirming that one is free to judge them as such, that one can judge and not create a new version. The relativist is then the one for whom the problem does not matter.

It is very possible that the purpose at the origin of the ethno-psychologists' research—to go toward "others" in order to know "us" better—was to better deconstruct our own knowledge in reflexive contrast with other conceptions. But if the ethno-psychologists were able to constitute a "twelfth camel" for Vinciane, it is because they learned to take the full measure of what their approach implied and to make themselves worthy of it. In itself, this approach bears witness to the fact that they belong to a tradition where the meaning of emotions matter. Is it not this tradition they are prolonging when they accept the demands of their research, namely learning from the encounter with the emotions of others, at the price of clashes, misunderstandings, frustrations, even humiliations? For not interpreting the emotions of others, but conferring to others the power to make perceptible the difference between their emotions and ours forces self-exposure to the (emotional) experience of this difference.[2] And via the politeness by which they sought to encounter the others' experiences—not one

2. A number of ethno-psychologists recount their malaise, their feeling of being displaced, sometimes their suffering, when the difference of emotional experiences, which were precisely the object of their research, abruptly broke in an unexpected way into the relations with those they had decided to live with (on this subject, Monique Jeudy-Ballini, "Voir et regarder," *Gradhiva*, 15, 1994), pp. 59-74.

of them would dream of submitting the Ifaluks or the Bedouins to the deconstruction which accompanies the return to "us"—the ethno-psychologists learned to extend this same politeness to their own tradition, which is ours.

Let us not be mistaken, this politeness did not, under any circumstance, arise from a reflex of prudence, benevolent tolerance, or hypocrisy. It responded to a necessity to which these researchers have submitted their practice. And this necessity situated them as the heiresses to what it was no longer a question of deconstructing, but of prolonging, re-suscitating, and renewing, a tradition for which emotions matter to the point of leading us to go interrogate others, to ask them to place us in another kind of relation with ourselves, forcing us to produce new versions of our emotions. It may be possible to say that, like the twelfth camel, these versions allow a retroactive and not a reflective glance at the conflict between themes.

Nevertheless, contrary to the fable which ends with a successful division of goods and the return of the camel to the wise man who had gifted it, a necessity of thought takes on meaning here, which Vinciane has pursued ever since: that of "polite" versions, which are affirmed as such and ask to be evaluated as such, according to what they make perceptible and according to the way they are articulated to others, making them more interesting by stripping them of their thematic pretensions.

For Isabelle, the fable marked a path already embarked upon, whose starting point was a refusal which committed and situated her. Encountering a phrase written by a philosopher and feeling, saying, affirming "no" is not as such remarkable; rather this is what explains why polemics may take the place of thought in philosophy. However, in this case, it couldn't be a question of polemics. Because the philosopher in question was none other than Gilles Deleuze, through whom she had discovered a love for philosophy, thanks to whom she had learned that philosophy can be life-giving, irrigating zones of experience she had considered outside of thought, or that she didn't know existed. And because the phrase did not concern an interpretive point, but philosophy itself, namely what philosophy is committed to. In *The Logic of Sense*, Deleuze wrote, in parentheses: "see Leibniz's shameful declaration: he assigns to philosophy the creation of new concepts, provided that they do not overthrow the 'established sentiments.'"[3]

The qualification of "shameful," in the lexicon of Deleuze is anything but anecdotal. It is radical. Certainly, it does not impose the vocation of overturning established sentiments upon philosophy, like a ball in a game of skittle. But it nevertheless implies that these sentiments must above all "not be respected." Moreover it is addressed to Leibniz who was certainly a master in the art of respect, but of a respect with surprising effects: established sentiments, respectfully translated by Leibnizian concepts found themselves separated from their polemical power, the power to wage battle against other equally established sentiments, to the disarray of the battling protagonists. Deleuze was thus condemning not a "respectful" philosophy, in the sense of submitting to evidence and established sentiments, but a philosophy which seeks to reorient rather than run counter to, to civilize what we inherit rather than prolong the polemics to which this inheritance summons us.

Leibniz failed. He only succeeded in making the protagonists he was addressing agree on a single thing: that it would be a shame for them to accept the proposed translation. It could be said that Leibniz ventured to call into question, not theoretically but practically, the most ferocious of our established sentiments, the one that implicitly united these protagonists. All of them recognized truth by its polemical power—a truth is only

---

3. *The Logic of Sense,* Gilles Deleuze, Ed. Constantin V. Boundas, trans. Mark Lester, Charles Stivale (New York: Columbia University Press, 1990), p. 116.

worthy of the name if it can serve to identify and engage in the struggle with the illusions or errors it denounces. Leibniz, a mathematician, may have thought that the belligerents would accept a solution that articulates positions which had up to then been defined as contradictory—isn't that what makes mathematicians happy? Inheriting from Leibniz is admitting his failure without passing a judgment on it, and especially not drawing any conclusion from it (since he failed ... we may claim that ...). Rather, all this has to do with Woolf's cry: if it happens that, here or there, we are capable of thinking that peace is possible where conflict mesmerizes us, and reduces us to impotence, "think we must."

The fable of the twelfth camel intervenes here. It doesn't promise a miracle since the solution made possible by the added camel responds to the brothers' choice to "give peace a chance." But this good will is not at all sufficient. If we must think, to think here is to create, and that's what the old wise man whom the brothers consulted did. He immersed the asked question into a "space," as mathematicians say, endowed with a supplementary dimension, one which corresponds to the unknown which retroactively becomes part of the question: all right, it is a question of dividing up the inheritance, but upon what does the distribution key bequeathed by their father bear upon? Creating the problem, not accepting it as it is formulated but daring to add new dimensions to it, so that its answer is not that which, sadly, seemed decreed in advance, that was what Leibniz had done with his strange philosophy, with those monads which seem to belong to the arbitrary imagination of speculative philosophy. To understand them as something other than arbitrary is to understand what they make possible.

But how do we inherit from Leibniz, and also from Whitehead—another mathematician who became a "speculative" philosopher? It is here that we discover anew that our colleagues are right. Neither one of us serve philosophy, which does not mean that we just use it. Rather, we have the impression that it does not ask to be served, in the sense that one would defend its privileges, its territory and its great problems. Both of us would probably fail the philosophy section of the baccalaureate exam. Are we "true philosophers?" Maybe, in the sense that, like the sons of the old Bedouin, we are, and more precisely, we want to be, oriented by an inheritance where a leitmotif keeps coming back, the question that inhabits us, "how to think?" But not at all if to be a philosopher is supposed to mean drawing up the image of a thought that defines imposters and traitors— sophists, relativists, pragmatists, and other opportunists.

Both of us were opportunists and we knew it well— and moreover it was made known to each of us: where is your "oeuvre?" Why are you such "amateurish" dabblers?" But from now on, we can make the claim in a more impersonal mode, touching on the exercise of thought. We are women engaged in a man's profession, a profession which numerous men, as our predecessors, satisfactorily demonstrated to be unsuitable for women. If the question is "how to inherit?" this profession, then it cannot be resolved in a general way. A twelfth camel cannot be postulated. The creation of a slightly different version, which separates belligerent "themes" from their pretention to define the landscape, cannot be theorized. It is a grace, a gift, not the mark of personal genius.

We are opportunists because what we care for, in order to treat our objects well, demands not only that we sense they are poorly treated. We firmly believe that when the way a problem is posed puts us up against the wall of "either ... or ...," it is because the problem is poorly posed, taken hostage by "established sentiments," which dismember it. But trusting in the possibility of posing the problem, if not well, at least better, is a question of encounter, always "here," never in general.

It is not the place of philosophers to offer the supplementary camel to their epoch, like the wise man of the fable—philosophers are not wise people, and moreover, no one comes to consult them. Rather, we think that the camel belongs to the epoch itself, in the mode of what it is capable of becoming. We are not heroines of thought, braving established sentiments, but speculators of the possible, depending on the possibilities of thinking which belong to the present. And we do not serve philosophy, because success, for us, is that the twelfth camel can disappear from the scene after having served his purpose. In case of success, the page is turned, the habits of thought are modified; others will be able to take up the baton.

Virginia Woolf composed a work of memory—"to not forget," because that which had excluded her, and her sisters, was still there at the time she wrote *Three Guineas*, even if women were henceforth accepted into professions. In our time, when equal opportunity has become a slogan, we also must remember, because the exclusion of some men and women and the mutilation of all men and women continues. The contrast between the struggle, which must refuse amnesia, and the exercise of thought, which demands trust, is sometimes difficult to endure. But most of all, we must not say "either … or…." Either Martha who works or Maria who listens. This is a trap. We must never forget that this world makes struggle a necessity, that nothing here is "normal," and we must never stop thinking together, cultivating insubordination, including towards our own sentiments, each with the others, through the others and thanks to the others. Moreover, is this not the very meaning of feminism, this adventure which must be again and again reprised anew?

8

TWO PLUS ONE....

We thus discovered together, one with the other, through the other, thanks to the other, a shared sense of how this "twelfth camel" united us but that also opened us up to questions that we had never worked on. Words changed meaning, Amateurism ceased to be an insult. We remembered that the word has love, *amare*, as its root. A rather special kind of love, indeed, which does not dream of fusion—but rather of the creation of a relationship with what makes the singularity of what one loves. Yes we were opportunist amateurs, shamelessly meddling in fields where our authority was not recognized, called by the feeling of possibility, by events that awaken the sense of adventure where dilemmas seem inescapable. And we asked ourselves if we could fabulate that love "as women," as part and parcel of a struggle for what is living, for what asks to live, to branch out, to connect, rather than for the truth, if that truth demands that the other be recognized as conquered.

But we were already more than two. A third woman had joined us, long enough to give us a beautiful gift, a woman philosopher whose book one had entrusted to the other because she remembered that it was in that book that she had discovered the way in which Leibniz had intervened in a theological quarrel, the "Querelle du pur amour", the quarrel about disinterested love. Leibniz had advised that when love is concerned one should consult women, who are the competent ones on this subject. But what Vinciane took from the reading of this book, written by Émilienne Naert in an already distant past, was astonishing. Would women also be competent when it is a matter of inheriting from Leibniz, of loving Leibniz? Even more amazing was the fact that the traits chosen by Naert drew an image of thought similar to the one we had, together, started to explore.

And surprise, surprise, Émilienne quoted this famous phrase about established sentiments that should not be overthrown,[1] this time in its context. To produce certain new truths without overthrowing ancient ones but by explicating them more completely, is exactly what geometers are doing, Leibniz argues. And he thus defends himself from innovating while what he really presents in this text is his most scandalous proposition, that of God's choice to create, among all the possible Adams, the one who was going to sin. Following Naert's proposition, one can add to the reference to geometers a reference to alchemists, for such is the praise that Leibniz gives Locke: that he was not only one who tested things, that is, a critic assaying the gold in the propositions of others, but also a "transmutater"; he not only separated the good from the bad but himself produced "good metal" from what others were proposing.

Geometer or transmutater, isn't that how one could describe the old wise man with the camel? Refusing to make a clean slate, but constructing a version that would not be a refutation, in this case does not demonstrate a

---

1. Émilienne Naert, *Leibniz et la querelle du Pur Amour*, (Vrin, Paris, 1959), p. 27. The source of the phrase is not given in Deleuze, and in Naert the reference is wrong, but close enough that the mistake is correctable. It is a letter to Count Ernst von Hessen-Rheinfels, dated April 12, 1686. The Count, a Catholic, served as a relay in an exchange with the theologian Arnauld on the subject of *Discours de métaphysique* that Leibniz had just published, and in particular about the consequences of his notion of the individual for original sin.

shameful caution but a resistance to choosing the easy way out—your father was delirious, or he wanted to make you understand that you were free to interpret his will. The will is to be explicated not overthrown.

Leibniz is also resisting the authority always claimed by the one who presents himself as a free agent with no strings attached. "All those who wish to appear to be great personages and who set themselves up as the leader of a sect have something of the buffoon about them. A tightrope walker would never let himself be attached in order to prevent a fall; if he was attached, he would be sure to succeed but he would not appear as a skillful artist."[2] Leibniz accepted to be attached, wanted to be attached, constrained by what those whom he addressed held to be true. A mathematician's truth, but also the art of versions rather than the claim to exclusive truth associated with the theme—he transmuted, translated, explicated, unfolded, and at the same time betrayed, in order to dissolve the power of the theme to impose a position against others as well as the power to fabricate sects that are assembled for the war over what Woolf called abstract ideals. Wouldn't these ideals owe their semblance of life to the opposition they incite?

Another citation from Naert: "I find in History that sects are ordinarily born through an exaggerated opposition made against those who had some particular opinion, and under the pretext of preventing Heresies, one creates them [...]. When one wants to suppress them, by the great noise that one makes about them, by the persecutions and the refutations, one is trying to extinguish a fire with bellows."[3] Leibniz knew that ideas become Causes in whose name massacres are committed. In a similar fashion, Whitehead, after having celebrated *The Banquet* where Plato co-defines the soul

---

2. Leibniz, unknown date, probably to Electress Sophie of Hanover (Gehrardt IV, 295), cited in Émilienne Naert, *Leibniz et la querelle du Pur Amour*, op. cit., p. 28, note 46.

3. *Ibid.*, p. 31, note 55.

and the Idea—the enjoyment of the Idea being what puts the soul in motion, what makes it feel and think—concludes: "It is obvious that he should have written a companion dialog which might have been called "The Furies,"[4] dwelling with the horrors lurking within the imperfect realization of Ideas.

The Leibniz of Émilienne Naert can close this chapter because she proposes to us a version of our inheritance ignored by philosophers who only see hypocritical protest in the way Leibniz defends himself from being an innovator. It is perhaps not coincidental that it is a woman philosopher who provides the portrait of a Leibniz "sincerely" attached to a thought that would not be polemical. Without a doubt, it was important to Naert to give full meaning to the singularity of this philosopher who, far from "shutting women's mouths," proposed that they should be addressed about the most important problem, that of the love appropriate to give God. Thanks to Naert, we can in fact understand the meaning of Leibniz's advice to the polemicists: if it is a question of speaking about love, it is necessary to trust the experience of women because they are competent in the matter. And they are competent not because they are "carried away by feelings." Speaking to women, to those "femmes savantes" of the epoch, whom Molière ridiculed, implies neither condescension nor "essentialism." Could we go as far as to make Leibniz – the master of abstraction, who made of abstraction a politeness of thought and of politeness a constraint on creation, and who was, as such, "marked" by ridicule—the prospector of what could be another "genre" of thought? For if women are competent in matters of love, it could very well be because of their attention to manners of doing, saying, and thinking. Because of their refusal of letting a duty to "speak truth" bar the road to "speaking well." Because they do not set themselves up as "leaders of a

4. Alfred North Whitehead, *Adventures of Ideas* (New York: The Free Press, 1967), p. 148.

sect" or claim to silence others but share a disinterested love of language and thought. If the "femmes savantes" have been for Leibniz the sign of a possible civility of ideas, where men were waging war in their name, his proposition could very well echo the question posed by Woolf when she wrote that we must think: "What is this civilization in which we find ourselves?"

In order to articulate our versions and our fabulations, we were already several, and it was time to go look elsewhere. Not to rediscover what the two of us had fabricated, not to repeat the kind of fortunate encounter that we had with Émilienne Naert, but rather to elude a repetition that confirms and ends up transforming a situation into an established position. If the fable of the twelfth camel still haunts the following pages, it will be seen from the angle of the trust that the three brothers decided to risk in going to consult the old wise man. Trust in the fact that the cry that made us think could find other echoes, induce other responses, no doubt divergent, but all situated by the question of this "civilization" in which we find ourselves.

But going to look elsewhere also meant inventing another kind of equality between us. For if one of us has frequented thought for a long time, the other was more familiar with fieldwork and with "*dispositifs*" aiming at an activation of thought, and in this case, aiming at activating a possibility to think with us. Our "field" would therefore be women who in one way or another might have encountered our question and could give it dimensions that we could not foresee. Women whom we felt could be competent concerning the situation we are trying to think, whose experience could help our own, who could add other stories to those we have woven.

To the three letters addressed to Woolf in *Three Guineas*, we have thus added a fourth.

PART TWO

Dear (...)

In her *Three Guineas*, Virginia Woolf was addressing "daughters and sisters of educated men" at a time when professions and universities were beginning to be opened to them, and she warned them to be on their guard. *Think we must*, she wrote, if we don't want to limit ourselves to the ambition of joining the procession of men charged with the honor and responsibilities from which our mothers were excluded. Certainly, today this procession is no longer quite what it was—it may have even transformed into marches of professors on strike. But in no way do we feel that Woolf's phrase has lost its full relevancy. Some 70 years later, we would like to ask these questions: what have we learned, we who have in fact joined the ranks of "educated men?" What meaning do we give to Woolf's phrase today? And if "think we must," how can we reciprocally assemble some diagnostic elements on the subject of what "women do to thought?"

It goes without saying that the questions in the first paragraph which we (Isabelle Stengers and Vinciane Despret) ask ourselves and would like to ask you do not arise from any sort of "essentialism." They are inscribed in a perspective of gender, a perspective inseparable from practical, political, ethical, and aesthetic dimensions. And they are addressed to you not as a "representative sample," but because we are convinced that each one of you is in a position not only to respond, but also to do so responsibly, because for us it would appear that each one of you has taken up as an issue the question "what does thinking demand today?"

From the beginning, our question is inscribed in a book project that the two of us wish to write together. The idea came to us to propose it to other women and thus to make it a question of "terrain," not merely concerning the "terrain where we think" but also the "terrain that makes us think."

Among those women whom we address, some are already explicitly and actively inscribed in questions of gender; for others, the link between thought and gender might be less evident. Moreover, neither one of us immediately recognized the fact that certain things said nothing to us as a question of gender. We probably had to first try out their effects. The moment has come for us to try a re-evaluation of what happened to us, and to make the wager that, for all of you, this question, if it is not formulated thematically or theoretically, but addressed to your own manner of fabricating thought, might have a meaning, or take on a meaning, perhaps an unexpected one.

If you accept our proposition, it will be up to you to determine the way in which you would like to "populate" our terrain. It could well be by general considerations that will be precious to us and will help us to think, even if we will not refer to you in an explicit manner. We are not asking you for confidences, confessions, or autobiographical accounts. On the other hand, during exchanges that we have had with each other, we have realized that those "anecdotes," particular events, or perplexing problems marked the path by which each of us discovered what "thinking" could mean for her. If some of you choose to speak to us about journeys, events, or anything that you consider important for having affected your choices and your personal style of work and thought, these gifts will be attributed to you by name. The way in which each of you will intervene in the text will be part of the preparation ("cuisine") of the book—it will not be a question in any instance of reproducing *in extenso* your contribution. We are speaking even more of "cuisine" in regard to this book that we consider each one of the responses as offering a version of the problem that we propose; we are therefore betting on multiplicity and on composition, against the staging of contradictions and judgmental postures.

We address this letter to (...). We do not doubt that certain among you will note omissions, some flagrant, but also the names of women who are less known (French-speaking, that's the limit we set for ourselves) for whom the question could be interesting. Do not hesitate to transmit our letter to these women or to send their names to us.

Furthermore, some of you might prefer to meet with us—possibly out of time considerations, but also, and maybe especially, because you feel that the manner in which we pose the problem should be discussed. It would be a great pleasure and interest to meet with you.

(...)

The formulation which announced our appeal was deliberately made to open a question, not to define a request. We did not specify what each of the terms used might signify. "Women," "make," "thought": we could not be more indefinite as to what we were expecting. The only clear point is that it concerned thought, not philosophy, and that it was to Woolf's cry that we were entrusting the possible ability to incite those women who would carry it on. We were therefore addressing women whom we thought were in a position to situate themselves as Virginia's heiresses, for whom thinking was not a means but what was at issue.

Thought, as what is at issue, is what both of us received from philosophy. We received it as a gift, a demanding gift, not as a right or a privilege. And perhaps the fact that we are Belgian took on its full importance in this case. For historical and institutional reasons, philosophy is not for us the queen of knowledge as it was not so long ago in France. It does not occupy that privileged position, which allows or allowed until very recently, the understanding that the non-philosopher is someone who lacks something. In our country, "you're not a philosopher, you can't understand," is only heard as a joke uttered by non-philosophers, when a philosopher proffers an abstruse pronouncement. Belgium, in this regard, is quite resolutely on the side of the serving girl of Thrace,[1] and the choice to engage in a *cursus* of philosophy (of which all are ignorant before coming to the university) responds to many motivations (notably the absence of math coursework) but certainly not the choice of a Royal Way.

Our choice to engage with the question of thought as an issue was thus not a diplomatic way of coopting women who "would be worthy of being philosophers." Addressing other women for whom, we believe, thought is an issue is nonetheless a form of cooptation. For there are many practices that imply thought, but they do not imply that "how to think" is a question that matters, that makes one hesitate—that makes one think.

When a scientist, male or female, although we could equally say a photographer or a talented cook, thinks,

1. This is of course a story that we were taught in philosophy, and that relates the fact that Thalès de Millet, preoccupied as he was in observing stars, fell into a well, causing his serving girl to laugh.

when he or she hesitates, when he or she doubts or hopes, what makes them think, hesitate or hope is what makes them a scientist, photographer or talented cook; these are the questions that convey the meaning and the stakes of their practice.

Because, each time the danger of a hierarchy turns up, denials are ineffective, we would like to evoke an experience that made us feel what we have just affirmed here. To make people feel is of course the meaning and the stake of works called artistic, and it is indeed a film, *Babette's Feast*,[2] that made us feel how the preparation of a meal might, for an exiled cook, put into play the very meaning of her life. Certainly, this meal that she prepares is a replica of those which made her famous in Paris; her gestures are confident, not marked by hesitation. Each one responds to what the artistic work in process demands. But what Babette is going to offer to those Protestant puritans, with whom she is presently living, is not the demonstration of her talent. She does not want to initiate her hosts into the "pleasures of the flesh," whose ascetic life makes God the sole source of joy, but initiate them onto another path to joy and grace. Turtle soup, blinis Demidoff, quail in sarcophagus, all moistened with an exceptional amontillado: her guests oscillate, all through the meal, between disapproval and surprise, reserve and emotion, distrust and welcome acceptance. For Babette, it is the very meaning of her life that is in balance. Will the work of love, which for her is cooking, have the power of a saving grace, even here where it is defined *a priori* as corrupting, as an outrage to Christian virtue? Her life is in balance until that moment of grace when words come to the guests to speak of an experience that they didn't know was in this world. Babette, who will never again recreate this work of art

---

2. Danish film by Gabriel Axel (1987). This film was inspired by a short story of Karen Blixen (Isak Dinesen), part of her collection, *Anecdotes of Destiny*.

on earth, will "enchant the Angels."[3] "Mercy and truth have met together, and righteousness and bliss have kissed one another!"[4]

But Babette's feast, no more than the experimental success that makes the physicist dance or the Q.E.D. which fills the mathematician with joy and admiration, or the image which resists the critical eye of the photographer, does not make high stakes of the question "how do we think?" All men and women think but what makes them think is inscribed in multiple modes of practice which each time determine the stakes, successes, possibilities of failure or servility.

It was therefore not, certainly not, a question of selecting the "elected" but rather those women who could relay Woolf's cry, "think we must." For them, "how to think?" is not an abstract or reflexive question but is inseparable from what in their case is creative work, practice, and engagement.

3. Dinesen, Isak. *Anecdotes of Destiny* (New York: Random House, 1958), p. 68.
4. *Ibid.*, pp. 60-61.

9

CONSTRUCTING THE QUESTION

Nevertheless, our formulation, "what women do to thought," said nothing about this. For us, it was a question of intrigue in the sense of leaving the question wide open in order to allow for multiple possible translations, which would not only be multiple versions of responses to the question, but also of the question itself. We wanted our correspondents to be intrigued, so they would be able to wonder (and they did): "But what do they want of me, those two women?" In such a way that their responses would take an active stance in regard to the question. We didn't explain what we wanted. We made no pronouncements on what thinking meant. Nor on what we meant by "women", by the way. The term "do," as the first dictionary we grabbed states, has a multiplicity of meanings, resembling a Swiss army knife; one "does" with it what one wants, according to the task.

The manner of responding to the question was supposed to translate the way in which each woman would construct it, would appropriate it, even resist certain possible translations. We want versions to proliferate and participate in the art of reconstructing the problem differently, of creating divergences with regard to the way it was framed. We were not inquiring, but attempting to produce what we had already experienced: an induction that gives a problem which that doesn't yet exist, the power to recruit those who will bring it into existence.

One of us had already experimented with this type of proposition, though in a slightly different way.[1] For a long time, the classic form of inquiry where the interrogated person must respond to questions that she had not asked herself, even recounting her life to someone who will make an argument or material for analysis from what she has confided in him, troubled her, even tore her apart; she had explored several more or less satisfying variants. Until she created a situation in which the participants in the inquiry—breeders in this case—were not confronted with questions but with a problem. They were asked how, according to them, the question should be formulated to correspond to the problem of the inquiry.

It was not a question of a methodological trick. The two investigators, in this case Vinciane and the sociologist Jocelyne Porcher, truly needed help. Each had a slightly different problem, but in both cases a problem that was rather difficult to share as such with the breeders. Vinciane wanted to explore the problem of the difference between animals and men, a problem which mobilizes many academic fields, such as philosophy, psychology, psychoanalysis, and anthropology, fields where this is usually disputed in terms of identifying "the human exception," with a remarkable lack of interest or curiosity with regard to animals. "Human exception" already says a lot about that. Interrogating breeders, therefore, seemed like an interesting idea—and, let's admit it, a way of interrogating the legitimacy of informed discourses. But who says the breeders will find this question interesting? Who says that it is pertinent? Who says that all these sweeping judgments about animals aren't

---

1. Vinciane Despret, Jocelyne Porcher, *Être bête* (Arles: Actes Sud, 2007).

merely tributaries of a question that can only concern academics? Why bring breeders into this mess?

For Jocelyne, it was a question of finding out if animals, in breeding situations, might be considered as working. Jocelyne Porcher surveyed breeders for more than fifteen years; the question had meaning for her. In fact, she remarked that a number of breeders evoked, though implicitly, mostly anecdotally, the fact that animals took an active part, even initiatives, in relation with their breeders' work. If this is the case, shouldn't we envision the relation of man and breeding animal as collaborative, where animals and people work together? But when she posed the question directly to the breeders, they gave her blank looks: no, it's the people who work, the animals don't work. What to do with the numerous anecdotes that say the opposite?

One solution was thus imagined for the two problems: it was necessary to ask the breeders to help the investigators to construct their questions. We would not address a "breeder," but someone who would respond "as a breeder." Each one thus recounted her problem and her difficulty: "We are not sure that our problem is of interest to breeders, or that the questions we are able to formulate are pertinent for them. Thus, according to you, as a breeder, how should we construct our question so that it has a chance at interesting those to whom we ask it and a chance of receiving interesting answers?"

In this case as well, a form of cooptation was involved, since the investigators did not address themselves to "a" breeder, but to someone whom other breeders had indicated to them (and this was made explicit) was in a position to reflect with them on the question of how to address "breeders"—someone to whom the question "how to interest a breeder?" would be interesting. This situation which recognized/made "experts" of their interlocutors, in regard not only to their practice but to their relation with other breeders, was accepted as such and yielded answers to the question that they had not formulated. For, of course, by constructing the question in a way that would interest breeders, the breeders responded to it as well; better yet, they constructed interest in the question, and their responses were enormously interesting indeed. Each interview brought its share of surprises, exhibiting the creative dimension of a process which assembled everyone's intelligence: breeders, cows, pigs, investigators. The question, as it was reprised and reinvented in other terms by each breeder, already coupled the practice of the inquiry with the art of producing versions, versions which interested the breeders enough that those of them who came to understand the trick of the starting point—it was not at all a question of "preparing" a survey—nevertheless gave recommendations of other breeders "to whom this might be interesting."

Our "fourth letter" attempted to create a rather different situation, however. With the breeders, it had been a question of learning how to better communicate with people whose interests did not necessarily correspond with ours, learning the pertinent questions from them and with them. It was not a question of bringing a "we" into existence. Some breeders spontaneously evoked the fact in the course of the interview that, "now that you make me think" and "really reflect on it," they had seen their own position change. But that was not the goal, even if it showed that the experience felt by the investigators of having thought "with them" had been shared. Our fourth letter did not recognize our addressees as "experts", persons to whom we could write: "We are addressing you 'as (...).' X, whom we have already met, suggested to us that you would be susceptible, and perhaps interested, in helping us." As what, in this case? As a woman for whom the question of "how to think" matters? That would be really vague and even insulting for those women that we didn't choose. Moreover, it was not a question of thinking about the formulation of a hypothesis with them but to have them experiment with a proposition, the meaning and consequences of which should be determined by each one, in her own way. From this point of view, our letter was functioning as lure, but lure may be interpreted as aiming to trap as well as aiming to create an appetite. And it was not for us to take away this indeterminacy, for it was part of the risky hypothesis which we tried out, that of a possibility of saying "we." But this "we" was mostly mute about the women it would bring together. It was situated only by the first paragraph—Virginia Woolf's warning and the question of the meaning that this warning can receive today. We were thus addressing those women for whom access to university studies and professions is not simply progress, or the disappearance of an anomaly, but especially to those women for whom Woolf's injunction— today like yesterday, again and always, think we must— would produce effects of relevance. It is the meaning of an induction—the "we" in question does not determine those women who can recognize it as relevant but exists only if it produces effects of relevance.

How did we select our correspondents? No criterion could prevail since the stakes were not "to construct a question," but to prolong the induction which had already contributed to the modification of our own relationship to thought. We were not even constrained by the criterion of a "university career," for Woolf addressed all women for whom their university education would open up access to the "procession of educated men," access to institutions from which their mothers, today our grandmothers or great grandmothers, had been excluded. We have thus functioned "by guesswork," "around us," a little like the breeders who recommended others with words such as "that one, he should...." We have also searched our memories and asked for advice. Knowing well that rather than being an inquiry, ours was a speculative attempt to induce, suggest, infect. In order to learn. In order to prolong what had started as a journey for two.

10

AN INDUCTION, IT'S WORKING....

... Or it's not working, and the fact that it is not working is then registered, without the slightest judgment. Some of our correspondents did not respond; others promised to do so, but the response never came; some, and this was rare, answered us in a style with which, rightly or wrongly, we could do nothing. In all these cases, there are no grounds for speculation—a lack of time played a role, certainly, but time is lacking so often when one experiences difficulties in situating oneself in relation to a request, when perplexity predominates. And the question is even more opaque when we don't know at which moment in their lives this proposition reached our correspondents. Induction is a little like luck, which one cannot seize if one is not ready for it. It has no way to insist, only to solicit.

Certain non-responses or barely disguised flat refusals are more easily read. On the one hand, there are women for whom our question had nothing to do with an induction because it directly concerned what already made them think. And in this case, the indeterminate character of the solicitation must not have induced perplexity, but rather a certain fatigue, as if we were asking them to write an activity report, or an article, one more. *Who do you take yourselves for?*, some certainly wondered. We understand them all too well, even if we don't adhere to a cumulative perspective ("that has already been done!"), even if we believe in the practice of reprise, of relay, of repetition under conditions which are a little different each time. On the other hand, certain women responded in a such a way that they made obstacles to induction perceptible. They were already committed, and it is their very commitment that created a determined resistance to our proposition.

Such was the case for Françoise Sironi,[1] whose life and practice are traversed by what categories, borders, and summons for identification do to people. For her, the proposition, "think we must" is already fully activated and "how to think?" fully in play. But it is in a style which does not lend itself to the hypothesis of a "we," however deliberately constructed it might be. Today Sironi works with people who call themselves transsexuals, who ask for surgical intervention but do not seek a reassignment of their "authentic sex." It is the assignment itself which was the dirty trick, a trick "think they must" in order not to continue to suffer the effects. And the memories of Françoise Sironi are those of a birth on a border— that of Alsace between French and German territory— and a relationship with an Alsatian grandmother who changed her nationality four times and always refused to speak the language of the "others," and with an Italian grandmother who secretly learned to read. If thought was vital to Sironi, it started with the refusal to think and be thought about in the thought of others. "As a

1. Françoise Sironi is a psychologist. Educated in ethno-psychiatry, she directed the Devereux Center, founded by Tobie Nathan. Her first field of research and practice concerned political victims of torture, as well as the torturers, and it is there that she learned to define her therapeutic practice as a work of restoration of thought (Françoise Sironi, *Bourreaux et victimes. Psychologie de la torture*. Paris: Odile Jacob, 1999). She participated in the founding of a rehabilitation center in Russia for veterans of the wars in Afghanistan and Chechnia, and has written *Psychologie des violences collectives. Essai de psychologie géopolitique clinique* (Paris: Odile Jacob, 2007). Her last book is about her work with transsexuals, *Psychologie(s) des transsexuels et des transgenres* (Paris: Odile Jacob, 2011).

woman," for her, is like a residence assignation, while thought means liberating oneself from the assignation, from the territory which claims to speak through you.

As for Géraldine Brausch, she is certainly one of Woolf's daughters, but what engages her corresponds more to the verification of what Woolf had predicted: if women join the "procession of educated men," they will become like them, will look with the same scorn on others who are excluded. The formerly "ignorant women," states Géraldine in her answer, are now really legitimate inhabitants of a territory where knowledge is foremost a question of sorting out and selecting, which can be defined only through the waste it produces. For her too, it is necessary to think, and on the terrain designated by Virginia herself: what are the modes of production of knowledge which create exclusion? And it is necessary to do this where we are, that is to say, for Géraldine, in the world that is hers, the university. Perhaps it is because her engagement situates her in a world she must affirm as hers in order to resist that Brausch forbids herself from fabulating, that she asks what difference women have "really made." Thinking in front of the scorned women, the wasted lives, forbids what appears to be a sort of detestable double-dealing— right, we are no longer with you, we have successfully played our cards, but we remain "different."

Marcelle Stroobants[2] offered us two successive responses. We will come back to the second, but we will quote the first here because we read it as similar to Géraldine's and Françoise's: situated by an engagement that would present an obstacle to the induction. In her case, it was through her engagement in her field, the

2. Marcelle Stroobants has been left-handed since pre-school, discovering, while she was at it, an interest in technical devices, ways of getting along and animal strategies. In 1968, sociological studies became the obvious choice for her as well as for many students at the time. Then the experience of wine harvests served as the providential springboard toward the sociology of labor, a research perspective with a broad spectrum and the principal subject of her teaching at the Free University in Brussels. A list of her publications can be accessed online, which does not include all of her forthcoming projects.

sociology of labor: a field where it is necessary to do battle again and again, and not for the pleasure of triumphing over an adversary but because good will propositions, appeals to a "true" knowledge, which would transcend opposition, are a trap. For when it is a question of labor relations, if "think we must," it is in order not to forget that the wage relation is constructed. To forget that would be to forget that this construction has been, and will be, as long as capitalism exists, inseparable from collective struggle. This is perhaps why we have interpreted this first response as a warning. In this field, the "as women" enters into dangerous resonance with "relational competences" or with a "gift" attributed to working women as corresponding to a "natural vocation": to be attentive to others, "to be care-givers," even to sacrifice themselves. What counts for Marcelle Stroobants, what "she wants and must think," is this cry, "Neither maids, nor idiots, nor nuns." ["*Ni bonnes, ni connes, ni nonnes.*"] This chant came out of the collective intelligence of nurses on strike. The hand may be soft, but it is a question of finding or rediscovering its fist. What goes without saying, if it is a question of vocation, must be said and claimed when the wage relation is concerned. And the fact of saying it, of rediscovering one's fist, Marcelle insists, signals the possibility of the recognition of the professionalism of the caring gesture and modifies the relation to outside judgment: *The reaction to the "what will people say" is radically transformed, appeased.*[3]

It could therefore be said that Marcelle's first reply is not only a warning, it is also the proposition of a promising example, which permits her to situate herself as a sociologist of labor interested in the question of gender. Rather than let themselves be locked in to the alternative of refusing or claiming a difference peculiar to women, the nurses forced recognition of what, in fact, their profession demanded. And the difference therefore

3. Here and later, we have chosen italics and not quotation marks to indicate that we are quoting our interlocutor.

is no longer either a privilege or a trap: women are not born nurses, some become nurses, and this becoming, the learning of the art of "caregiving," must also be accomplished by men who are engaged in the profession.

Confronting the responses that we read as "no, thank you," left nothing to argue about, to insist upon, or to defend ourselves against. These are different versions of the "as...," articulated with different causes, situated by a different "think we must" that, in return, situate ours in the mode of fragility. Yes, the "we" that we have fabulated did not predate our journey, and it is fragile, almost ridiculous, in relation to what, in our worlds, is endowed with a much stronger power to make people think, act and struggle. If we were preoccupied with a thematic truth, with a version defining the others as rivals, we should bow down. Not acknowledging fault with feminist struggles (post ..., queer) but with the manner in which we passed the baton. But the versions are nourished by the meeting with other versions, which diverge without contradicting because each one produces its own terms. Affirming this fragility suits us— after all, what orients us is indeed this fragility of those women who have been there where, for Woolf, "one should abstain from going."

The first effect of these answers was to remind us that, from the moment when we undertook learning via writing together, our proposition was inseparable from the journey; we had to retroactively acknowledge the experiences that situated us in relation to Woolf's induction; that is, to acknowledge, come what may, what we had done, and how the letter we then sent situated the others in the same terms.

Other responses that we received have further disclosed the particularity of our journey, this time in regard to what it ignored and of which these responses reminded us. Not that these experiences they gave voice to are foreign to us, on the contrary, but it was probably necessary that others re-suscitate them so that we, in turn, might recognize ourselves within them and through them. The answer Laurence Bouquiaux sent us could be read as a way to respond to us, but also to respond, at the same time, to Woolf: the doors of the university may well have opened to women, and those who answered us may very well have benefitted from this opening; this does not mean that they feel "in their place" there, that they have not encountered the kind of experience that feminists associate with the "marked" gender.

11

LAURENCE, MAKING A PLACE FOR HERSELF?

The letter from Laurence Bouquiaux[1] begins: *I was inclined to respond to you that I wouldn't respond.* She didn't see how her response could have avoided participating in the usual cycle of complaints and bitterness. *I risk inflicting on you my habitual jeremiads about what I should have done and what I didn't do, perhaps mixed this time with something like "if I had been a man"... that is neither interesting nor convincing. But something happened that made me want to write to you.*

We will come back to what happened, but its first effect was that Laurence, in her letter, does not complain. Rather, she expresses in lucid and merciless words what we all know. She situates herself among those university women for whom "making a place for oneself" first of all comes down to finding oneself in a place marked by the risk of feeling, or being made to feel, "out of place." She evokes the *good female students, hard workers, even grafters, who know they are tolerated as long as they remain inoffensive. Leave the talking to men (at meetings, conferences and even, perhaps, in books) because many of our colleagues*

---

1. Laurence Bouquiaux, mathematician and philosopher, teaches philosophy of science and the history of modern philosophy at the University of Liège. She recently published with Bruno Leclercq, *Logique formelle et argumentation* (Brussels: De Boeck, 2009).

95

will only pardon us for being intelligent if we renounce being brilliant. Modesty is a cardinal virtue (for women, of course). We get things done, we wisely apply what they taught us, but if we invent, it's on the margins, regarding questions without prestige that men would not spend an hour on. Nothing very amusing in all that.

Even less amusing when the reminding slap is never far away. And to top it off, we who have not really adopted a modest position, know perfectly well, having lived it, what Laurence is talking about: *The big names of the faculty, as it must be, are all men. It is not astonishing that a man who adopts a position, saying he's deeply shocked, and makes an appeal for equity and intellectual honesty and academic dignity is a man who has a sense of universal values; a woman who does the same is hysterical.* We know this experience all too well, and we know at what point it becomes poisonous for it is essentially insoluble. Certainly, it happens that one receives a reminding slap when one had thought one was in one's rightful place, but it is always possible to wonder retroactively if there was not a reason for inviting the slap—something in my voice, my attitude, my tension "marked" that I did not feel completely "in my place," and authorized the reaction that signaled to me that I wasn't, indeed. The insolubility of the chicken and the egg, one could say, between what one feels and what others make you feel: that's the very meaning of this notion of "marked," when the mark is accentuated in a place where you are supposed to have escaped it.

How can we be astonished when women, as Bouquiaux stresses, often spontaneously adopt an inoffensive position: a humiliating position for a man, completely acceptable for a woman, one that the institution encourages beginning with the first years of university study. *As if women do not feel authorized to contest, to argue, to take a position, or only in a very soft manner, in the form of a question or suggestion that they let be understood, already in formulating it, that they would be ready to give up.*

96

They don't think about it any less, but, in most cases, they will drop the matter more easily than men.

To feel out of place and to nevertheless have gotten a place, accepting right away the mark that assigns you to a docile and submissive attitude, Bouquiaux stresses, is the temptation of "parvenus," *those who did not "stay in their place," who are occupying places for which they had not been destined. Is the position of women fundamentally different from the situation of those who are not the sons of educated men and of whom one doesn't expect that they have the class or elegance of those who fell into that situation when they were children?*

The parvenu is also the traitor, the one who, because he feels "out of place," flaunts his exemplarity, this time in the terms of "I did it," even "if I did it, why can't others?" The parvenu is a product of the situation that stabilizes this situation and, from this fact, breaks with the possibilities of solidarity and resistance. Feeling out of place, for a woman, may have for its result to side with the rightful owners of the places; it is in relation to women that those women who have passed to the "other camp" have to disassociate themselves. *At the time when I was trying to read Leibniz's texts on infinitesimal calculus, I participated one day in a round table discussion with Pierre Bourdieu. It concerned, among other questions, the fact that certain objects of study were typically masculine and others typically feminine. As an example of the first, I remember that Bourdieu had taken the "mathematics of Leibniz." The colleague seated beside me told me, laughing hilariously, that he didn't know that I was "a drag queen." I admit that I felt a certain (and stupid) pride. On the other hand, I would have found it insulting to the nth degree if someone said to me "ah, it's good that you study that, that's a fine subject for a woman" or "it can be seen, by the way you approach the question, that you are a woman."*

We will return to the reason why Laurence decided to give us this merciless analysis. But we want to proceed here with a stark contrast. Among all the women who

97

answered us, one presented herself in a mode which could very well overturn the accusation of "parvenu." The parvenu is one who needs the recognition of others to authenticate the fact that he "did it." For Françoise Balibar universal knowledge is a "gay science," a knowledge that she learned (from women) had no need for special recognition.

12

FRANÇOISE, A FEMININE "GAY SCIENCE?"

When I hear women complain about the difficulties they have encountered from the fact that the knowledge claimed to be universal is in reality masculine, I don't understand what they are talking about. For me, the universal was first of all feminine. Men had success, technique, efficacy, social prestige; but "true" knowledge, the one acquired, the one that liberated, the one that the educational institutions of the period valorized in high schools, the gay science, has always been feminine. As a girl, it always made me feel at home, welcomed, yes welcomed. To the point that while later evolving into a world of scholars persuaded that they represented the universal, I did not feel like a fish out of water: their universal was also mine, even if for me it had been initially presented from the aspect of the feminine. To the point that I have the impression, or rather I am sure, to have never been exposed to masculine hostility: men have never put a spoke in my wheel ... at least not in the domain of knowledge.

It was from her mother, who had an advanced teaching degree in physics and who taught at the high school where she herself studied, that Françoise Balibar[1]

1. Françoise Balibar is a physicist and historian of science. She directed the CNRS team which produced a six volumes Selected work of Einstein In French.

99

learned what a gay science or knowledge demanded, those virtues that Woolf attributes to the daughters and sisters of educated men and that Balibar reminds us of in her letter: *These virtues comprise "chastity" (which, transposed to the professional domain, leads to the proscription of all forms of the prostitution of the mind for money), "derision" (that is, not according any value to medals and other baubles whose derisory aspect must remain obvious) and, finally, independence vis-à-vis imaginary loyalties that ruin the lives of those who think they are real; no backsliding, no national patriotism, no old boys' clubs, no cliques, no mafias.* And it is also her mother who gave Balibar *the hardest lesson, but also the most salutary, that I have ever received in my whole life. One day, in high school, as we were getting ready to return home together, I started to display, with self-importance, some newly acquired knowledge, in the same tone as my father, that of someone who thinks she knows, but who, it is clear in the eyes of those who really know, should realize everything is much more complicated. Then I saw appear on my mother's face that famous disapproving pout that had up to then been reserved for my father. And, as we were passing one of her colleagues, she let loose in a revolted tone, intended to express her anger: "My daughter is a prig!" I learned that day what the word "prig" meant. Ever since, even today, I have dreams in which my mother looks at me with this expression of strong reprobation. By dint of reflecting on this episode, I have concluded that the important word in this address is the word "prig," because of its meaning, certainly, but especially because of its grammatical gender, masculine, which makes it difficult to accord with the subject of the phrase "my daughter." I had just performed a reprehensible act from the point of view of true knowledge and the punishment that my mother had spontaneously found was to exclude me from the feminine. It was as true for her as it is for me that thought in its most complete and universal form is configured (*dargestellt, Freud would say*) by the feminine.*

For Balibar, then, it was men who were associated with the figure of the parvenu—in this case, the "bling bling" figure, the one who showed off his wealth, while the "true rich people," the heirs, pouted. And when she describes herself evolving into a world of (male) scholars "persuaded that they represented the universal," there is perhaps the hint of a pout, but the touch of irony is not polemical; rather, it is indulgent. Knowledge is universal, even if the relation to this knowledge may be debatable.

And yet Françoise Balibar has not avoided the feeling of being "out of place," or worse, "excluded:" *The exclusion of the feminine has poisoned a large part of my existence.*

It is the very happiness with which she evolved into knowledge, the way in which she felt "welcomed", which *very quickly appeared suspicious to me. As a girl, I should not have felt at home in what, outside the universe that my mother and I formed (possibly extending to the Marie Curie High School), everyone (almost) considered as belonging to the masculine. I can understand (today) that this apparent facility of evolving into a world reputed to be masculine might enrage women who have spent all their lives trying to make themselves heard by men assumed to be possessors of knowledge, itself assumed to be universal. If I suffered from this hostility, it's because it's aim was accurate: it awakened in me the fear, discovered in adolescence, along with sexuality and desire, of not "being" a woman, at a time when the words "woman" and "man" designated two genders just as antithetical as the grammatical masculine and feminine. Two "identities" defined by distinctive criteria forming a coherent ensemble, among which, in those debates about feminism (the 1960s), the domination of men over women in the domain of thought permitted, through transfer of the dominant/dominated division, the foundation of the man/woman distinction; feminism, in its beginnings, believed to have found a non-essentialist criterion, a political criterion there. And in my corner I told myself that there was something "abnormal" in not feeling oppressed in the domain of thought, something which cast doubt on my identity as a "woman." I was 18 years old and I did not yet know that it is impossible to construct a coherent sexual identity following the feminine or masculine binary.*

Françoise Sironi would speak here of a "dirty trick." With discreet simplicity, Balibar speaks bitter-sweetly of the necessity in her situation to *"cobble together an identity that didn't make me suffer too much, an identity of a "woman" conscious of not corresponding in every particular to the supposedly coherent list that defines this word—and to accommodate herself to it.*

However, not everything has been said, for what Françoise Balibar did not also perhaps yet know at the age of 18 is that it may well be impossible to construct a coherence between the virtues of the gay science and a university career. *I asked myself the question of knowing if I should have followed the advice of Virginia Woolf* (Think we must) *and reflected on it twice before letting myself be seduced. Still to this day, I have no answer to this question—which after the fact, in in any case, hardly has any meaning.*

The question has even less meaning in that Françoise Balibar refuses to give a particular value to her own disappointment. What has been betrayed is not the confidence of someone who believed that the university was true to this gay science to which the feminine world of her youth had initiated her. If the virtues that Woolf associated with knowledge are not current at the university, *nothing allows me to think, 70 years later, that women have behaved better than men in this regard. The most one can say is that these virtues (whose subversive value Virginia Woolf probably exaggerated) are today valorized by both men and women: everyone would like to work less, cultivate friendships, take one's time, enjoy the moment when the moment demands it; everyone condemns intellectual prostitution, cliques, and patronage. But since, in fact, nothing has changed, the conditions V. Woolf insisted upon have not been realized and the question of knowing if it is proper to join the dance is again being posed.*

Françoise Balibar's letter, so generous in its sincerity, is even more troubling in that her own path from physicist to historian of physics seems to demonstrate the choice to sidestep the cult of speed and competition and the desire of recognition of those who "represent" the universal and fight in its name. And it's not a coincidence, certainly, that the book that she consecrated in 1993 to Einstein and his work (of which she directed the annotated translation at the CNRS) is titled *Einstein. The Joy of Thought.*[2] Einstein, for Balibar, is the one who is not a prig, the one that her mother's disapproving pout would have spared. Apparently Balibar's choice did not however carry with it the possibility of nourishing a living rapport with the gay science.

Here we could return once again to the words of Françoise Sironi when, in her own answer, she tells us of the necessity not only to construct an object, but also, especially, to "treat it well," *to make it live without the institution killing it.* Is it because the "object" to which Balibar consecrated herself is also an object of veneration for the procession of physicists that she has today started to wonder if she shouldn't have reflected twice before joining this procession? Is the joy of thought sufficiently nourished when she participates, even against her will, in the cult of a great man?

Françoise Sironi has harsh words that resonate here: *It's a trap; you think you're adding a stone to the building, and you only add to its rigidity.* For her, the case is clear: if "think we must" concerns the university, it is in terms of the *modus operandi.* Because entering the university is one thing, but *once you are inside, they will look for ways to devitalize you.* It is necessary to construct one's object, but especially *to protect it, to construct the means of its non-destruction,* for the "dirty tricks" will begin. And there, Françoise, who doesn't even want to speak "about women," joins Marcelle in recognizing a particular vulnerability in them when one appeals to their devotion, their loyalty to the institution: *I have a colleague who did what was necessary, who made herself indispensable, who accepted administrative tasks that no one wanted—and she drained herself. And the worst thing is her bitterness, her*

---

2. Françoise Balibar, *Einstein. La joie de la pensée* (Paris: Gallimard, 1993).

resentment against the women who were capable of protecting themselves.

It is time to return to Laurence, who would not have answered us if she had not felt capable of something other than the "regime of complaint and bitterness," this very regime that signals what Sironi calls "devitalization." Something happened which made her want to write us.

13

LAURENCE, THE COURAGE TO RESIST

"It made me want to write to you," these are perhaps the words that indicate the success of the induction that our letter attempts. The induction is not a suggestion for it proposes a taking up of the baton but does not say how to do it. It modifies the sensitivity and, for Laurence, it may have offered a somewhat particular accentuation for an experience that had nothing *a priori* extraordinary about it. For it concerned one of those routine moments of academic business, a Faculty vote to decide between two candidates for a teaching position, in this case between a man and a woman. A banal event. Except, she tells us, that during the vote, the vast majority of the women voted for the woman candidate;[1] which had been a surprise. *As far as I know, there had not been any preliminary meeting "between women," no watchword sent out. But it's a little like something had been awakened, even in all those women who, in general, are resigned to the situation. A regret and/or a certain admiration for those women who resisted.*

---

1. Without going into details, Laurence estimates that four out of five women and less than one of every two men supported the woman candidate.

The outcome, however, seemed settled, for the male candidate was working on subjects whose importance and legitimacy could not be questioned, serious, *a man sure of himself, steady, very professional, thirty-two years old but spoke like he was fifty, handling the academic rhetoric perfectly. He had been expected forever and he knew it. A career efficiently managed. Already all the honors and all the signs of recognition. Well deserved, no doubt. An uncontestable legitimacy and moreover uncontested.* In short, a candidate of perfect appropriateness with the criteria of the procession of educated men, and whom the procession was getting ready to welcome as was very normal. Against him, a woman researcher, who chose more marginal objects, objects she loves and protects, to which she learned to respond and from which she learned to follow what they demanded in order to be well thought about.... And two women were supporting her, *with much courage, and, let's say it, efficacy,* although neither of them was *accustomed to taking the floor in solemn assemblies.*

Against all expectations, the woman candidate won. If there was solidarity among the women, it was largely unconscious, *but that's even better,* Laurence writes us. For what differentiated the candidates was first of all a certain relation to knowledge, a certain way of thinking, and this difference gradually infected, first those who defended the woman, then a majority of the faculty members (including quite a few men), with the sense of the possible, to protect against the probable. A possible that Laurence had not imagined for a single second as having something to do with the dichotomy of man/woman. *However, in thinking about it again, it seems to me that the attitude of the candidates, their objects of study, the comments that the faculty debate elicited, then the vote, all that was indeed marked from the point of view of gender.*

The fact that an event of this type suddenly begins to matter to Laurence Bouquiaux, and to matter not as a surprise but as inscribed in the register of gender, is that linked to our induction? It could just as well be said that it was the event that gave meaning to our question and conferred it with the strength of an induction, which revitalized resistances and made Laurence want to write to us, to put our question to work. Did the event happen at the right moment or did our letter? We don't have to choose. A chance is created and is seized. There is, as she writes, something that was awakened and engaged in resisting. Moreover, it's the same for the vote of the faculty members. Laurence Bouquiaux doesn't know if it shows regret for all the times that they didn't resist, or respect those women who, this time, resisted and gave others the courage to do so. It could even arise from both, it doesn't matter. What matters is that there was resistance, even from those women who had previously been resigned to doing nothing. Her choice in writing to us was to transform into an event what could have been easily reduced to a mere anecdote *which deep down changes nothing.* She asks the question: *What makes one adopt one attitude or the other? That one chooses resistance or resignation? And how does one sway to the side of resistance those women who have chosen resignation? When they resist, women are magnificent! Like this single word carved in the stone (on the edge of a well, I think) in the prison of Aigues-Mortes where Protestant women were incarcerated: "Resist."*

14

BERNADETTE, GIVING
HERSELF PERMISSION TO THINK

If there is a connection between the women who answered us, however, it is not situated in a difficult relationship to the institution. For Bernadette Bensaude-Vincent,[1] *what was hardest was to give myself permission to think, to claim to be an author, responsible for my words.* Bensaude-Vincent's answer speaks to us of a path marked by the determined, obstinate refusal of what so often serves as prosthesis: one exists because one crosses swords, because one is recognized by the others with whom one crosses swords. It's for this that young people are educated: *The intensive coaching for dissertations posing a well-defined problematic and offering a solid response after several rounds of argumentation,* that's what may largely spare many from what was for her *the hardest.*

However, if giving herself permission to think was so hard for Bernadette, it's not, apparently, "as a woman," but rather because, very early, she had access to the joy of thinking, of being overwhelmed by this joy, thanks to Michel Serres with whom she worked as an assistant.

---

1. Bernadette Bensaude-Vincent, professor at the University of Paris 1 and member of the IUF, dedicates her research to history and philosophy, and the history of science and technology: chemistry, material science, nanotechnology. She is also interested in the relationship between science and the public as well as current thinking regarding a "politics of innovation."

His thought was contagious. Of the two hours of lecture in a Saturday class, I only heard the first half hour; after that, I was scribbling my own thoughts, constructing chapters of my thesis in an effervescent state.

We will not say that thinking "by contagion" is not thinking. But it is running the risk of letting oneself be carried away without creating one's "object," the one which, in return, will set one to work. *Serres did not teach me the craft,* and it's with a true historian of science that Bensaude-Vincent learned this craft, a historian who was *meticulous, in love with details, so careful that he hardly dared to hazard new concepts, yet willingly polemical; he launched me into interminable historiographical controversies, arguing every inch of the way, demanding. For the first time I was "chosen," my thought was recognized as worthy of being discussed, and at the same time I was recognized as a woman worthy of affection. He was the one who gave me the serene confidence necessary for embarking on the writing of a book without knowing where the writing would lead, just to see.* Arguing every inch of the way, here, is not crossing swords, for those men and women who argue in this way are situated by a shared question: they are "colleagues," in the etymological sense of the word, brought together by what forces them to think: for historians, by the archives which one must not make say what one wants them to say.

However, for Bernadette Bensaude-Vincent, the craft was not sufficient, for in addition, she had to have *the joy of finally understanding, of no longer always being carried away, banging about, because there is a way to pose problems, of seeing differently, that suddenly changes the landscape.* Moments of being, *this beautiful discovery by Virginia Woolf, I have sometimes rediscovered it in moments of mute thought. Feeling traversed by the flux of generations, not like "dwarfs on the shoulders of giants" but as a full member of a collective movement to which I may belong for several years, one or two decades. Three little turns in the whirl of ideas, of forgotten books revisited. This right of passage into the collective being of thoughts constantly being reworked, given up and re-appropriated, I acquired it thanks to two events. The first is the encounter with a theme that I can call my own: the materials, our daily partners, mute and too often scorned except in emergencies; the other event is less unexpected, programmed as it was by a biological clock. Menopause liberates us from the servitude of the need to please or at least to be attentive to the glance of others. It is also the time when one is liberated from the daily care of children. The education process—in spite of all the effects of happiness that it evokes—confers a certain gravity to the slightest gestures. This is something serious. We have known since Antiquity that philosophy is the daughter of leisure. It is hardly compatible with worry, constant care.* Care leaves hardly any freedom to think.

We were surprised by this "less unexpected" second event, since whoever knows Bernadette Bensaude-Vincent would not associate her with that from which, she says, menopause liberated her. But here we find a trait common to those who accepted our question and who perhaps verified that for them "how to think" as such is at stake: lucidity, for them, does not refer to generalities but always to a journey. If menopause is part of the journey, we must think with that, too. We cannot keep ourselves from evoking all those moments when one realizes that, "here again," what spoke through ourselves was the fear of being poorly perceived, the desire to be appreciated, that, here again, we laughed with the others even though there was nothing to laugh about, that we let ourselves be recruited. "Carried away, banged about," who has not known these somewhat shameful moments about which it's not a question of being dramatic, but which women, perhaps more than men, know to take note of, know to keep the memory of? Bernadette acquired her "right of passage" not into the procession but into the "collective being of thoughts," when she encountered her object and knew that she would not prostitute it, would not make of it, even involuntarily, an instrument of seduction. And the way in which she connected the two events that permitted

111

her to "take her place" reminds us that Iroquois women, past the age of rearing children, took their place in the council of women where vital questions were decided, including war and peace. And also that, for the witches of yesterday and today, the third age of women is the one that gives them access to their full powers, the one when, formidable or welcoming, haughty or warm, they discover the serenity that makes them "guardians of wisdom," that is, also, crones.

Still, the allusion to menopause was very brief. We wrote back to Bernadette, who answered us: *Certainly, it is not a question of praising menopause, but it liberates us from an assignation that is less hormonal than cultural. For one lives the biological condition through what language says about it. No longer having my period does not displease me; no longer being "indisposed" means being both more poised and more available. Even more, it means getting out of the obligation to "appear feminine," to play an appropriate role, to dress appropriately and wear make-up, etc. One finally feels liberated from the stereotypes of femininity. This discussion brings back a memory from my youth that I had completely forgotten: "Don't lose your femininity," the headmaster of the Joffre High School in Montpellier said to me when I applied, at the age of seventeen, for entrance into* hypokhâgne. *These preparatory classes are reputed to transform candidates into "library rats" or pimply assiduous nerds. They are certainly not places for the good life, but one can flower there, yes, learn to dance lightly in the middle of the procession of educated people. Menopause liberates us from the worry about responding to the expectations inspired by the stereotypes of femininity. It installs a new gender that is neither neutral, nor masculine or feminine, as French grammar would dictate. Nor is it hermaphrodite, even less "unmarked." It would rather be a "white gender," at the age of white hair! But this white is less a lack of pigmentation than the sum of all colors. It is the possibility of changing colors as the events propose.*

We are not renouncing either the Iroquois or the witches, for Bernadette gives us another version which is not contradictory. Following the whim of the events, accepting the events, not seeking to bend them to stereotypes but knowing how to listen to what they propose and what they demand. Even *hypokhâgne* can become a proposition for freedom, a light dance with knowledge that does not yet impose the question of what that means, to enter into that world, to take one's place among those men and women whose books one discovers. But the subtle grace of irresponsibility does not have the seriousness of assumed responsibilities as its only correlative. What Bernadette learned, with the deliverance that she associates with menopause, is rather a freedom that no longer needs the protected space of preparatory classes, the freedom of this white capable of responding to the event. Wouldn't this white be the color of the becoming that fabricates what one calls the "vieilles femmes indignes," shocking old women, those who give themselves permission to laugh and escape assigned roles, those who can no longer be counted on to do what was assumed they would always do?

15

MONA, DON'T DENY

W hen Bernadette introduced menopause into the journey of her life and thought, she dared to raise one of those questions that can cause anger because they are apt to evoke the idea of a "biological determinism," even of a "feminine nature." But for Mona Chollet,[1] avoiding such questions, even denying them, is unfortunate, even if feminists are not wrong to distrust references to nature. The current state of affairs proves them right: *I am rather perplexed by the movement today that sees women, in the name of the very real difficulty of the working world, abandon it to dedicate themselves to their families, preferring to be financially dependent on their partner. Similarly, the current vogue of ecology and the revalorization of "nature" are also leading to a re-naturalization of sexual roles, to a return in force of traditional clichés about the "natural" vocation of women—maternity; and the critic of*

---

1. Mona Chollet is an author and journalist (*Le Monde diplomatique*). Among her published works, notable are: Mona Chollet, Gébé, *Marchands et citoyens, la guerre de l'Internet* (Paris: L'Atalante, 2001); *La tyrannie de la réalité* (Paris: Calmann-Lévy, 2004—republished in Folio Actuel, 2006); *Rêves de droite. Défaire l'imaginaire sarkozyste* (Paris: Zones, 2008); with Olivier Cyran, Sébatien Fontenelle and Mathias Reymond, *Les Éditocrates, ou comment parler de (presque) tout en racontant (vraiment) n'importe quoi* (Paris: La Découverte, 2009). She also writes online analyses tying together politics and culture on the website "Périphéries" (http://www.peripheries.net).

the "will to control" is leading some to call abortion rights into question.

For Mona Chollet, such revalorizing of the domestic universe and housework is a trap. And it is not enough to stress that if so many women struggled to escape the role that was devolved to them, it's because the "work of care" *was the responsibility of women alone and they exhausted themselves with it.* The small problem is that *this critique never ends with men being enlightened, a sudden consciousness-raising, and deciding to work part-time in order to assume their share of domestic chores with pleasure!*

In order to escape this trap, however, is it necessary to deny the question? Must we deny a difference which is not necessarily natural—no more so than the effects of the onset of menopause may have on a life? Must we bend ourselves to abstract loyalties that would prohibit women from making allusions to hormones in the name of all those women in whose faces these hormones have been thrown? How to avoid the "revalorization" of nature, the "re-naturalization" of roles, except by separating this reference to "nature" from all moral connotations, but also from all power to dictate a role? The "natural" is not what's coming back full force, or maybe it is, but in the sense that it is an idea, whose power is that of an abstract ideal. As for "nature" itself, in the sense that those who observe the multiplicity of inter-sex arrangements among animals could testify to, let alone the multiplicity that prevails in definitions of the "biological" difference between a man and a woman, a qualifier is imposed: *queer*—strange, bizarre—that is, disconcerting. But it is only disconcerting to those who are looking for a norm. Scientists who are called "naturalists" learned early on to marvel at the way that "nature" thwarts their expectations. Nature has made them into raconteurs of amoral but delightful stories.

It is perhaps in this way that Mona Chollet would like to see a distinctive women's culture recognized. A culture whose values could refer to the dominant culture in a mode of resistance—while the men squabble over abstract ideals, women laugh in the kitchen and exchange knowledge with a coarseness that would frighten many men. *Among these denied and repressed values,* Mona Chollet continues, *I would cite for you, pell-mell, a greater capacity to envision the human being without opposing nature and culture, without absurdly denying the presence of nature in humans nor feeling humiliated by it; a capacity to think in terms of connections and interdependencies, rather than isolated and distinct objects; a capacity to think and to write with the greatest possible honesty toward oneself and others, without being afraid to put one's own doubts and weaknesses on the table, without worrying about adopting an advantageous posture, or about demonstrating one's allegiance to an intellectual "club" which has at its core the protection of its funds of commerce. This may authorize putting one's least glorious aspects on the table, or what, in the eyes of others, simply has no possibility of becoming material for serious thought.*

This is perhaps what we were looking for, in writing this fourth letter—the frankness of responses that would not be confessions, for even if it is a question of what could seem "least glorious," the women who write to us are not intending to "confide" in us but to bring us material for thought. It seems to us that Woolf's cry, "think we must," will have to be reprised, over and over again, for as long as women don't cultivate together this capacity for which they have often been reproached, of being honest and able to laugh together when abstract ideals rear their head. As long as they painfully hesitate, each one alone, between two assignations, that of a "feminine vocation" and that of a refusal of any "feminine specificity."

16

BARBARA, ANGER AND LAUGHTER

Among those women who responded to our letter, Barbara Cassin[1] is without a doubt the one who hesitated the least. The refusal of any assignation is not what directed her response, but rather, one could say, a constituent part of herself. For her there is no privileged status in regard to thought. Not only in *what* must be thought about (when she writes *Voir Hélène en toute femme*, what gets her working, she says, is the beauty of Helen's dresses and she deliberately gathers together *the texts which have an effect on her*) but in the "what" thinks, what one is thinking with. *For me, being a woman is not believing in, nor wanting to incarnate, the difference of literary genres. When I write, I cannot believe that there is a difference between poetry, novels, philosophy. Nor is there a difference between painting, love, maternity. They take shape together, without limits.* Cassin will not even speak about aspects

---

1. Barbara Cassin, philosopher and philologist, is the founder of the Network of Women Philosophers at UNESCO. She has published many works of note, including *L'effet sophistique* (Paris: Gallimard, 1995); with Maurice Matieu, *Voir Hélène en toute femme. D'Homère à Lacan* (Paris: Les Empêcheurs de penser en rond, 2000); *Avec le plus petit et le plus inapparent des corps* (Paris: Fayard, 2007); with Alain Badiou, *Heidegger, le nazisme, les femmes, la philosophie* (Paris: Fayard, 2010); and *Il n'y a pas de rapport sexuel. Deux leçons sur «L'Étourdit» de Lacan* (Paris: Fayard, 2010). She was the chief editor of the *Vocabulaire européen des philosophies, Dictionnaire des intraduisibles* (Paris: Seuil-Le Robert, 2004).

echoing each other, for *to speak about echo already implies difference* since that assumes distinct materials between which a reverberation echoes. And not believing in this difference is also not declaring permeability, but practicing permeability, that mobile connecting of multiplicity that makes up one's life as mother, painter, poet, cook, lover, philosopher. This means resisting everything that would identify her, "you are, you are not," refusing to submit to assignations that require making a choice or that constrain her to the criteria of a particular field and its boundaries. *The boundaries always arise afterwards, they are drawn when one acts, they are not preexisting but produced, and they are produced in such a way that one can always put them back in question.*

When the boundary tries to be imposed from the outside, when it does not belong to what "happens" in the course of what is being produced and makes it necessary to take one path rather than another, the response is one of anger. *An example: early on, I wrote short texts—long poems and short stories—that I printed and published myself. In 1973, perhaps. A book which spoke about a poem, a pseudo-poem that resembled one of Char's poems but wasn't his. And the notes were other poems, printed in different typographical styles. I showed them to some philosophers: they said to me: "Ah, that's really very good. That's how you must write." But to say "that's how you must write" means "Damned little fool, don't do philosophy, it's not for you." Therefore, I could say that* L'Effet sophistique *is a product of that anger. Ah, I am not to do philosophy! You are going to see that I do it better than you.*

Anger is not a mere reaction, it nourishes a response. Barbara Cassin made her anger a force, an ally. It cannot be said that she mastered it; on the contrary, it should be said that she learned to be shaped by this anger, to fashion it into a force of impact. L'Effet sophistique *is the very impact of this anger.* Our tradition knows well that anger has an impact, for it has cultivated anger as something that comes out of ourselves and makes us accomplish things that can sometimes be affirmed, retroactively, as previously unthinkable. Certainly, in this same tradition, great anger, burning indignation, is rather the motivating force for men. For women, it is the anger of despair, not that which would inspire heroism in the service of great causes. But Barbara Cassin offers another version of women's anger, which she claims as such, as a woman. To the assignation "we know where you are," her anger responded: "No, I am not there. And if you put me there, I am going to look elsewhere."

It is always something in the order of anger that makes me draw together one action rather than another. It made me draw together writing rather than painting, philosophy rather than Greek, even though painting would have been easier than writing, Greek easier than philosophy. I did not choose the thing that was the most comfortable, natural, taking the slope I was inclined toward. I chose, and that's why I am a woman among men, what was in a certain way a proof or a test, being directed by the fact that I couldn't stand tests. At her *concours d'agrégation*, this crowning selection of those who "made it," she had produced a history paper for the philosophy exam, a paper on literature for the history exam. *I had it all wrong, happily, because I didn't see myself living in there.* Precisely because no permeability is authorized there.

However, not being able to stand it does not mean becoming a sacrificial victim; that would be giving too much honor to rules. When it is a matter of vital questions, it is necessary to do what needs to be done. And Cassin knows how to distinguish between tests that can be happily refused and moments when it is necessary to do what needs to be done. Within this difference, Barbara sees a strength that belongs to women: the strength of her mother, who, when the Germans came to look for her husband, answered them, "me, marry a Jew, never!" in a tone such that the Germans had no other choice but to leave. As for Barbara, in a moment of necessity, when her only chance for the future was her acceptance at the CNRS, she did not hesitate. Shamelessly, she did what was necessary, writing perfectly compartmentalized articles, this time, each one perfectly addressing the interest of one member of the jury. She got the position. When it is necessary, when it's a question of life or death, women excel, and men give in. *The ultimate demands are made by women, and they get satisfaction.*

For Barbara Cassin, to be angry, but to be nourished by that anger without letting herself be devoured by it, without transforming it into a virtue that demands sacrifice, certainly did not mean mastering it. Her mother had not mastered anything at all; she dominated nothing; the situation required her to exceed her possibilities. Once again, it's a question of permeability to what the situation demands. And for Cassin, the permeability of anger and laughter is vital. *Confronting a situation can be done only while laughing.* No grandiloquent heroism, just do what has to be done. *That trick, it's a woman's thing: it's not possible and it's possible in another way. These are the truest experiences, the most real that can be. To have thought pass through everywhere, that is true permeability.*

"It's possible in another way." For Barbara Cassin, protecting her objects against what Françoise Sironi calls "devitalization," and more precisely protecting what makes them animate, their recalcitrance to disciplinary fixations, is inseparable from a practice that is itself recalcitrant to the "serious" nature of the masters. *The opposite of permeability is mastery or anesthesia. But I clashed more with mastery than anesthesia. For you can escape anesthesia, it's not all that contagious. But you can't do that with mastery, it imposes itself, you can only angrily not give a damn, and I need to get angry so that non-mastery may be a position. It is necessary to affirm it with sufficient force for non-mastery to be respectable. Making non-mastery respectable has enormous consequences. There's something like panic in thinking differently: faced with panic, anger. But then, always, I laugh.*

In *Voir Hélène en toute femme*, Barbara Cassin didn't situate herself explicitly "as a woman." That would have been succumbing to the serious, to demonstration.

Theses on language and ontology and the question of what men are looking for are all linked together. You are performing, in writing Voir Hélène, *"what can a woman do?," but you are not thematizing it.* When one thematizes, one doesn't laugh. And her interest in the sophists comes from their avoidance of confrontation. Rather they disturb the universal, the oneness of the truthful discourse—they drive it up the wall.

Nevertheless, laughter does not prevent another kind of serious, a commitment that connects Cassin to the sophists. Protagoras knew that you can't make someone move from a false opinion to true opinion, *but you can make him move from a poor opinion to a better one* for *himself,* for *the community: it's a dedicated comparative.* The question is not what is true, but what is "more true" for a given situation, thinking from the situation, dedicated to what is better for that situation. *The dedicated comparative is well-understood relativism.* With the *Dictionary of Untranslatables,*[2] of which she was the editor, the dedicated comparative does not need to be thematized for it is at work in the hesitations of the translators, the solutions they must invent, always under the sign of the *better for here.* Translation, thus, as a passage from one language to another, from one universe to another[3], is again a way of disturbing the universal, but not universally—certainly, the transaction is universal, but it is a universal in transit. *That's my feminine position. It is not the imposition of the power and domination by the "one," Plato's universal. It is creating a place where you disturb the universal enough to make it advance. Critical relativism disturbs the universal to make it progress, and if you act as a woman, you disturb it even more.*

That is why women laugh, why they can and must laugh. For it is a question of disturbing, not of responding in a symmetric or ironic mode to the omnipotence of a discourse that wants to reach the principle, that wants to

---

2. *Dictionary of Untranslatables: A Philosophical Lexicon* (Princeton: Princeton University Press, 2014).

be the discourse on the things themselves and claims to be universal. *Someone said to me, life is a bear. You fight with it, or you watch it pass by, from behind a tree. As for me, that doesn't worry me at all that I watch it pass by, from behind a tree. The powerful discourse, man's discourse, I watch it pass by. The all-powerful philosophy—I never wanted that.* Laugh and elude the retaliative argument that makes thought a battlefield—if you engage in combat with me and it's not based on some sort of truth, you are like a barking dog.... If you are not a dog, fight like a man ... or a woman?

Watch the grand discourses pass by. As a woman among men, laugh, at the edge of the well, like the serving girl of Thrace. And like Cassin did, when she remembered that this same Thales, the one who was going to fall in the well, was affirming that everything is water, the first universal proposition, and died of thirst. But if Cassin is indeed the heir of the mischievous serving girl, she does not limit herself to profiting from the accident. She digs wells into which men of the universal will fall; she fabricates traps where they will catch their feet, in such a way that they will be unable to plead that it is their absorption in their relation to truth that makes them fall, for it is this relation itself that will have permitted them to be trapped.

And it is in an astonishingly similar vein of inheritance, that of a line of women who cultivate anger and humor in order to resist, that the response of Benedikte is inscribed. Except that for her the universal is not the theoretical universal of those who claim to speak in the name of "great problems" or in the name of Truth. Rather, it is the all too common universal that authorizes those who claim to speak in the name of others, or, a gesture of an even more fearsome violence, to know "for the others"—explain to them, in all generosity, what they—male or female—"represent," and what their words as well as their situation "really mean."

17

BENEDIKTE, DON'T FORGET

Explain. *One should abolish the word explain!* The violence of the one who claims to understand and who is going to explain is what Benedikte Zitouni[1] inscribed in the heart of her answer, a violence that she learned to recognize as inherent to the relation with knowledge as learned and practiced at the university. For Zitouni, in order to sustain a memory, to inherit from Woolf, she must refuse to forget that she and her mother were the women to whom explanations were given, the women from whom understanding was demanded. It is also, as a form of protection, to foster the malaise, almost anger, that this memory reignites each time. *So many men have explained things to us, my mother and I, single mother and only daughter, that I get goose bumps when people explain things to me. And especially if it's for my well-being. And even more when nothing has been asked. It does not matter: this explanation and its interest for us are taken so much for granted that it*

1. Benedikte Zitouni, urban sociologist, teaches at the University of Saint Louis, in Brussels. She is also a member of GECo (Group of Constructivist Studies) at the Free University of Brussels. She has recently published her first book: *Agglomérer. Une anatomie de l'extension bruxelloise (1828-1915)* (Brussels: ASP-Academic & Scientific Press/VUB Press, 2010). She also collaborated on the book *Usus/usures* (Brussels: Éditions de la Communauté française, 2010) and has published articles on urban ecology, on interactional studies of the city and on action led by the GIP (Group of Information on Prisons).

is delivered freely, magnanimously.... So many times, we, on our side, have politely nodded our heads, made some oohs and ahs indicating interest when we should have simply told them that if this was about explaining things to us, well, that didn't interest us, thank you very much, and goodbye! From then on, I found it indecent to permit oneself to explain things to others; explanation is a resource that I consciously deprive myself of in my work as a researcher and teacher.

Retroactive fabrication? Fabulation? Benedikte poses the question but does not resolve it; if it is a fabulation, it's in order to be able to inherit from it, to make it available for reactivation, to make the violence or rather, she says, the indecency, perceptible—in fact, *after the act, we don't lick our wounds but we ask ourselves, amused or annoyed, suffering from hallucinations in any case: "But how can they believe that we are so ignorant?"*

To maintain a memory of this experience is to choose to be bound by it. In her research on the history of the constitution of the city of Brussels, she had to remain constantly vigilant: *I would have liked to have railed against certain truths and declare what the city truly was, what the society was, in a way that was stronger and unequivocal and general, I sincerely believe that I had a penchant for that.* Re-suscitating the experience of the man-who-explains, reactivating the indecency, just like actively remembering that one is vulnerable when faced with this indecency, when one knows that one should say, "no, thank you, and goodbye" and one doesn't say it, this is, for Benedikte, choosing a mode through which she inherits and which binds her.

For me, personally, the confrontation with this attitude that must be repelled has constrained me rather than liberated me; it's a source of privation that has led me to do sociology in a rather factual and austere fashion. The style of the reports of my empirical data has become austere, perhaps a bit autistic, especially in order to avoid saying what others must think. I say austerity, privation, because each time that I start to give myself airs, larger momentum, truths, I must erase them because I realize that I am reproducing a violence that I cannot assume, I see a resurgence of the man-who-permits-himself-to-explain-without-anyone-asking-anything. But at the same time, in this factual austerity, I have also learned to dramatize the account: first, in order not to bore the reader; second, and this is very important for me, the reader must always feel that there is someone telling the story, who exaggerates the trait, who manipulates the data. There are certainly other ways to confront the man-who-permits-himself-to-explain, I am not saying that this is the best, but for me factual austerity + manipulating dramatization have been a way out. Even more so because I was constrained by the antipode of the man who explains, that is I had to assume that the reader had her own universe, many other acquaintances that I did not have. Austerity has been a way to respond to this positive assumption: I cannot foresee what she, with all her acquaintances, will be able to do with my text and therefore I must leave room for unforeseen connections and not predetermine them. I must bring an end to my account, that's certain, but I cannot predetermine its consequences and connections.

Accepting the constraint to "never do that" has thus committed Benedikte to bring together what are so often opposites: the facts, nothing but the facts, or the manipulating dramatization, which transforms the facts into a vehicle that can lead to a conclusion. It is not for nothing that one may speak of the "art" of versions, while the theme, the translation that is only a vehicle toward the meaning of the original text, has no need for anything other than "letting the facts speak," that is, making them say what the *modest witness*[2] heard what

2. The "modest witness," in the sense that Zitouni defines it here, responds to the way Donna Haraway defines it in "The modest witness: feminist diffractions in the study of science": "This self-invisibility is the specifically modern, European, masculine form of the virtue of modesty. This is the form of modesty that pays off its practitioners in the coin of epistemological and social power. This kind of modesty is one of the founding virtues of what we call modernity. This is the virtue that guarantees the modern witness is the legitimate and authorized ventriloquist of the objective world, adding nothing from his mere opinions, from his biasing embodiment. And so he is endowed with the remarkable power to establish the facts. He bears witness: he is objective; he guarantees the clarity and purity of objects. His subjectivity

they were obviously saying. To construct a version, to make a dramatizing gesture perceptible, would thus be to give facts an austerity that they themselves never have. To connect them in this way, to "make" them speak this way, but without validating "this way," so that they remain available for other connections.

To speak of the art of versions while speaking of Benedikte's style is to speak of a practice that affirms the conscious refusal of what one does without even thinking about it. But also of a practice that chooses its materials, which assures itself that it will resist treatment, that it will be capable of not validating an interpretation. *There are other words and attitudes that I consciously deprive myself of in my work: "it is only," "what they meant to say." As if, in saying these phrases, I was reproducing the attitude of the man who permitted himself to explain to us things that no one had asked him about. To the point where I had to abandon a practice that I had nevertheless loved* a priori: *interviews termed qualitative, conducted on the run and in the field. I have always had the impression that I was stealing words from them, from the interviewees, because I was noting what they were saying literally without them being able to reflect on this literalness, without them being able to construct their statements with knowledge of their purpose. Suddenly, because of this unease, I had to fall back on documents and stylized discourses constructed to exist in the world, whose existence the authors acknowledged and that I could then take seriously since they were acknowledged by their authors, whether male or female.*

This experience that Benedikte refashions, in the form of an always active memory, as a kind of tool of vigilance, a constraint of abstention which she made into a creative constraint, can perhaps be read as an inheritance "as a woman." It is indeed as such that she presents it or proposes to fabulate it in order to be able to inherit it: *Only daughter of a single mother confronted*

is his objectivity. His narratives have a magical power – they lose all trace of their history as stories, as products of partisan projects, as contestable representations, or as constructed documents in their potent capacity to define facts." *The Haraway Reader* (New York: Routledge, 2003), pp. 223-224.

with the man who explains. There are also, she mentions, *so many other things that one sniffles at a little quicker than the others when one is a female researcher, a daughter of: the patriarch (of the research center), the cocks (strutting their stuff in meetings), the polemicists (who think that the world is waiting only for their argument, their good word)....* So many repellent figures, which, in the end, it is not too difficult to avoid identification with—a little humor suffices. But the problem is completely different when one begins to teach. For in this case, the memory of the man-who-explains makes Benedikte sensitive to what is ignored via the abstraction of good will found within the pedagogical directives aiming to valorize "interaction" and the "participation of students." One has to act as if one was welcoming the knowledge and experience of students, but the dice are loaded.

This has practical consequences for the teacher: I never ask questions in the lecture hall that begin with "who knows?" or "who thinks?" because the silence that may follow makes me very uneasy. Of course they know, they know much more than I, but I have put them in too abrupt a situation, asking that they extract this small bit of information. Worse yet, they weren't asking me anything, and nothing required them to find the course interesting because it is up to me to try to get them to embark into my universe while always presupposing, still, that they know an enormous amount and that they too have their own universes, universes with which mine will perhaps connect. I find this a very violent way to interact with students during a course in the name of anti-hierarchy. As if, suddenly, the man was turning toward my mother and I, still nodding our heads politely, and asking us a trick question (from a position of entrapment since the question was asked by him, in his narration and his spirit, he has all the dates and data fresh in his mind) in order to be able to better establish his authority and to calmly continue his explanation. In the lecture hall, after class, it's an entirely different thing, because then the universes begin to meet each other.... Another consequence: I no longer ask any opinions about the authors or the books that I use because that places the student in a position of knowing less; they never really teach me interesting things because they displace themselves too much toward my position or my universe in order to try to add something more inside it: the whole business is once again a trap. Rather, very classically, I admit, I ask them to describe for me the universe that I tried to display and, maybe, to speak about its implications and consequences.

18

ÉMILIE, IT'S NO ONE'S PLACE

Teaching, *there is nothing self-evident about it*, Émilie Hache[1] concludes. And here again, it is a question of keeping the memory and a willingness to be constrained by a commitment. *Not self-evident* is, in Hache's answer, like a formula at once protective and affirmative. A formula whose effect, she writes, is to not forget the relation of gender, which is as much in play in the choice that she made of thought as in the situation of having to teach.

Don't take it for granted, don't consider that it's a question of something "normal," or worse, of something merited: *The "daughters of educated men" may certainly go to the university today, but for some of them, myself included, the relation of gender undoes this false evidence of being in her place there. Not in the sense that the guys would be more at home, but in the sense that this is not the place of anyone in particular, it's not "due" to anyone. While being there, I don't forget all those women and men who fought so that the following generations could go there, or those women and men*

1. Émilie Hache is a philosopher and lecturer at the Université-Paris Ouest-Nanterre. Her research concerns ecology in its political and moral dimensions from a pragmatic point of view. She has recently published her first book: *Ce à quoi nous tenons. Proposition pour une écologie pragmatique* (Paris: Les Empêcheurs de penser en rond/La Découverte, 2011).

for whom even today the university is inaccessible. This "it is not self-evident" accompanies me in the way that I teach a course and in the way I conduct myself as a professor vis-à-vis my students, just as it does in the way I write.

The relation of gender that Émilie Hache talks about is not only a relevant category in socio-historical analysis. It is a construction, certainly, but not in the sense where one could say "this is only a construction;" it is a way of situating oneself which exposes and obligates and which itself will never be assimilated as a given. *One thing that has obsessed me since I began to teach at the university five years ago, and which adds to the fact that choosing the profession of an intellectual, a philosopher, for me will never be completely acquired, it's also a constant question of knowing if and when I begin practicing my profession in a way I don't respect. It's a bit naive, but I don't believe too naive.*

Here, again, one can hear the threat of a "devitalization," but not only that, because for Émilie, the questions associated with gender may themselves become a "power-over." For it is indeed a question of a power, *a power which makes me share with certain people the fact of seeing what others do not see. [...] In this sense, this relation is to be feared like a spell that can destroy [me], prevent [me] from writing, from acting, from thinking, a spell that one day destroyed Virginia Woolf when previously it had made her "clairvoyant." Here the question becomes how to respond to obligations, to beings with which one must engage in a vis-à-vis, without letting oneself be destroyed by it?*

Nothing goes without saying for Émilie Hache. The awareness of gender relations, transformed into an obligation, does not itself go without saying. It makes one see or feel, and it doesn't merely concern a different perspective, a different way of "constructing" reality. It's the reality itself that is different. When she talks of beings that oblige and demand to be taken into account, it's not a question of objects of belief. The relation of gender is engaged in the very refusal to make "seeing differently" a simple matter of subjectivity. Does not the judgment "it's merely subjective," have something to do with the grandeur of Man, proudly resisting the song of the seductive sirens?

To think in the presence of beings, human and non-human, is a choice that engages and exposes. Thus Émilie Hache refers to William James and the way in which he, who had chosen to live, made it a duty to think about the meaning of this choice confronted with those who had committed suicide. There is, she writes, *something of the risk for life which is at play in this relation of gender*, a risk and a test.

My relation to thought as "having nothing self-evident about it" obliges me to write for "professional" philosophers as I do for non-philosophers, not in the sense of erasing the difference of philosophy, but rather thinking "under the test of the presence" of the latter. This choice of thought is for me something vis-à-vis what I have to "account for." That "it is not self-evident" prevents me—in part, not always, not enough—from appealing to thought in an all-purpose way, that is forgetting those in whose presence one speaks. When Virginia Woolf writes that we must think everywhere, on the bus, in the kitchen, in a parade, I also hear that we, who have entered the university, must think while confronted with the people who are on the bus, in the kitchen or in the parade. That what I write, I who have entered the university, who have made the choice of thought, does not make them feel shame.

19

BENEDIKTE, THEY WANTED MORE

Thinking in the testing presence of others? The test may have several meanings, depending, for instance, on whether the others, to whom one has to be "accountable," are those men and women to whom it is necessary to not bring shame, or those men and women who may cause shame. Perhaps another statement by Virginia Woolf reprised by Benedikte Zitouni could offer protective strength against the power that Émilie fears, for the "power-over" bear upon all those women who were thinking everywhere, in the bus and the kitchen, while watching the procession of educated men parade by.

They wanted, wrote Woolf about girls who struggled to have access to university study, like their brothers. And it is Zitouni who reminds us of the phrase, *they wanted*. For her answer came in two parts. First it was a question of what she couldn't do, what she refused to do: to explain, think in the assigned place of the other, but later, in the second part, it was a question of affirming, of re-suscitating what she calls an "*idée fixe*," an obsession. *When I think of that procession and the girls who were watching it from afar, there is this "idée fixe" that always comes back:* They wanted. *I confess that I am not so much*

135

preoccupied with knowing if we have become like them, those men, as I am really wondering what has been done with this desire to know, to learn, to be acquainted with those universes to which the university (the words fit well together!) gives access to or, at least, offers something to grasp onto. They wanted *and we have to give an account to them.*

"*They wanted* and we are accountable to them." In this second part of her answer, Zitouni's world gets populated. To the "man-who-permits-himself-to-explain-even-though-no-one-has-asked-him-anything" are now added those women whom Virginia Woolf memorialized and whom Benedikte Zitouni makes into a force. These women did not only want to enter the university. Certainly, they wanted access *but their hearts were still somewhere else, I think. They wanted to discover other worlds, acquaintances. I am sure of that. When women like those in Brontë's novels looked into the distance and wondered what one learns in those universities, when they wanted to be able to go into libraries and read those books, it's that they wanted to accede to other worlds of comprehension. As in D.H. Lawrence when women spend their time in the house but keep their eyes riveted on the horizon. As in one of Woolf's stories where she notes the narrowness of her world and wonders what it's like to know Greek, French, mathematics, or astronomy. Or another story, where the daughter of a peasant is fascinated by the tales that a traveler tells her. Like these farmers' daughters who were secretly reading books under their covers and dreaming about more. All of them, they wanted. They wanted more.*

Three Guineas may be read, and was no doubt written, as a call to resist the edifying history of a progress that would be that of "our society," to resist the idea that if girls can now study Greek and astronomy at the university, it corresponds merely to the normal situation, and that to recall that it was not always like that would be a proof of resentment, of pettiness. But Benedikte Zitouni wants to see herself as inheriting something that connects the past and the present, which will never be normal, not the past exclusion, rather what this exclusion makes

136

perceptible—as thirst makes perceptible the enjoyment of the encounter of water with the body. *One must be accountable to the desire. It is not a desire to be educated. One does not climb upon a rooftop for that. Nor is it a desire to accumulate worlds and knowledge. But I think it's a desire which arises from the sensation of a brain hurtling against the four walls of the skull, which wants more connections, articulations, and unknowns in order to make a better life, to better understand what one finds oneself in the middle of; it's a brain that knows these connections, these alterations are there, that they exist but that one can't do it all alone, that some women must help us.*

To be at the height of this desire, and also protect the vitality of one's own being, is to make oneself capable of looking into the distance, and not with the critical distance or somewhat aristocratic disdain of those women who will no longer be duped by anything. What would the woman who was climbing upon the rooftop have thought if her brother had told her: "You know, the university is not what you think it is, if you went there, you would be disappointed...?" But the situation has not changed so much, and for Benedikte Zitouni, keeping the memory alive of that girl on the roof, is, in the present, to know that she is there, perhaps veiled, perhaps gothic, in the auditorium where she herself teaches. *Because when one is not the daughter of an educated man, when one doesn't know what the university is, except through hearsay, when the university is in the distance, just on the horizon, then one has this naive idea but one which I think is nevertheless important: the idea of having the university open up for us other dimensions of understanding the world and other cerebral connections. In order to make a better life, I repeat, in order to make a better life.*

In order to make a better life: those women whom Woolf wanted us to be inheritors of, those who climbed upon rooftops, those who were reading novels, those who were questioning a traveler about other places, those who wanted to learn Greek, a language of another world and time, are still among us today. We can be ashamed of the way in which their expectations—more connections, more worlds, more universes—will be nourished. We can dread, along with Virginia Woolf, what the university will make of them. But here they are, and Benedikte Zitouni, writing to us, makes the connection that confers to their presence the force of an obligation to be put in practice. *In practice: I had not thought about this desire in this way before reading your letter with the procession as an initial setting (because desire, yes, I am somewhat acquainted with it). And it's new and fearsome for me, this confrontation, what that means for the researcher that I am. First, do I open up a connection or a world in my research or my teaching? I know that it's pretentious to say this but at least it's a constraint that should support us when we speak in front of these generations. Second, in spite of the doubts or the criticisms that I may have about the university, I don't forget the promise that it represents, the promise whereby we can evaluate our actions within the university. It's too easy to play with the promise in a blasé fashion as if we've seen it all before. Sure, we know that the university is rotten. Ok, but then where else do we look for these necessary universes that make life better: the connections, the alterations, Greek, mathematics? We shouldn't abandon ship too quickly. Third, do we stimulate each other in order to dare, to write, to attempt, to fabulate, so that new connections can be created?*

Perhaps it is with these answers divided into two parts, those of Laurence and Benedikte, that we understand a little better the meaning of this fourth letter that we sent, the kind of evidence that we had experienced about this dispatching, in spite of its overall incongruent character, leaving to the receiver the burden of having to situate herself, to give meaning to a question that really wasn't even a question. It was, as Benedikte writes, an "attempt," in order that new connections might be created, and not only with us, or among those who answered us. For if there is a common trait found in the responses that we have cited, it is that those who responded have never presented themselves "as (individual) women" but always in relation. We had written in our letter that it was up to each of them to determine the manner of "populating" this terrain that we were proposing. We added that general considerations would be precious to us, specifying that in these cases we would not attribute the answers to them by name. We have not had the occasion to do that. And we discover again, in the contrast made legible by this absence, that generality is not in opposition to the intimate, rather to what is always of the order of the event, of the production of an articulation. The terrain is populated with encounters, all personal, all political, deploying the multiple meanings of the equation, "the personal is political." If they speak of women, it was of those—a mother, daughters climbing upon rooftops, faculty colleagues, women thinking and struggling—who had transmitted to them not a model but a strength that helped keep this resistance to the appearance of normality alive.

Our correspondents knew that what they wrote could be reprised in another way. They knew it even more certainly that one motif unites all the letters, declining itself in multiple fashions: "It's like this. It could be otherwise." This motif marked our exchange. Maybe this is why they would sometimes mention that it was up to us to know how to hear them—and each time, it was indeed what we risked doing. The baton is being passed, and passed again in the other direction, and is creating, in its return to the sender, new connections, differed effects of induction—what do they want from us? And perhaps this "up to us to know" is appropriate to the "we" that both of us had fabulated about the unfaithful daughters of Virginia, the ones who did what she said must not be done. It is up to us, to each one separately and together, to discover how to respond to her, how to accept the question that she asks us.

20

MARCELLE, NOTHING FORBIDS

For us to know: if one of our correspondents has more or less explicitly put us in this position, it's Marcelle Stroobants. Marcelle, with her first response, suggested that we be on the alert. Pay attention to the *care*, to the "taking care," which is typically thought to be a gift, a "talent" endowed to women, a veritable vocation— taking care is so "natural" to them that there is no need to indicate it as a necessary qualification for certain jobs. The devotion of nurses is priceless; they can therefore be paid less. But a second text reached us with this title: "Neither gift nor dowry." And this text placed us in front of a *fait accompli*—as if she was saying to us: "Here is what your letter induced me to send to you, it's up to you to know if you can make something of it."

The warning found in Marcelle Stroobant's first answer had been that of a knowing sociologist of labor, one who knows that she must always remember that qualification is the stake of battles, wage-earners struggling to get a qualification recognized, employers always demanding more advanced qualifications, with no raise in pay. And the second text extended this theme since she wrote us that: *No science is set up to intervene in these battles; the criteria of salary differentiation are in no way "objectifiable" except by way of professional collective agreements regarding the more or less complex character of the task in terms of the wage it will be paid. The most researchers can do is describe the brawls, the state of the relation of forces, record the results, etc.* And above all, maintain the memory of how it could have gone differently: nothing is "natural" when it concerns wage-earners.

But this time, Marcelle recalled the meaning and constraints of her discipline in order to evoke an event, that moment 20 years ago, when she discovered that she could, without betraying these constraints, work on questions she had previously thought the sociologist she had become was to renounce: *How are living beings transformed? How does one learn to walk, to talk? How does one invent? How are competences acquired? How is "savoir-faire" transmitted? These are variants of the same question— how does one become?—a question which first of all arouses distrust. For these big questions reek too much of the* idée fixe. *Vaccinated at a young age against the misdeeds of interdisciplinarity, the sociologist is only supposed to indirectly approach these questions, starting with the way they are dealt with by others. I didn't imagine myself capable of escaping this territory via the most academic of exercises, the doctoral thesis. And I didn't expect to discover my question regarding learning through examining the question of qualification since I was attached to a sociology of labor that had got its fingers burnt when trying to define what competence "truly" is. It is only in retrospect that I see the two threads that could authorize the pirouettes. First of all, nothing prohibits one from intervening in debates at the heart of one's own scientific community, even if it means following a "nomad concept" that would pass through it. If one follows a constructivist perspective all the way to the end, then the effects of a construction become part of the territory to explore. Qualification, even if it is the product of a certain number of collective conventions (in every sense of the term),may have important effects in terms of competence!*

The disciplinary object of the thesis was precisely the critique of interdisciplinary propositions, precisely centered around "nomad concepts," in this case, those of competence and *savoir-faire*, terms which researchers began to use in order to identify "true" competences, beyond conventional definitions. *Once the sociologist of labor's mission, always a critical analysis, was completed, the thesis could have stopped there; however, a small cache of diverse sensations still remained: first, the discovery that, in several countries, the proliferation of the term "competence" (associated with "evaluation") was not only used in relation with work qualification, but also in the educational sphere, suggested that something more important was at play, an intuition that was confirmed in the 1990s; next, and above all, there was the conviction that the demonstration lacked a conclusion. It's one thing to confirm that qualification is something that is not technically determined, that it's a more or less negotiated, conventional construction, however one still had to consider how it then produces effects of competence. In other words, if this construction is conventional and political, there is more to it than that, since it is bound to produce effects as well. At first glance, I was venturing into the uncertain domain where my cognitivist and pedagogical colleagues were leading me— the acquisition of* savoir-faire, *the formation of competences, apprenticeship. However, if qualification intervened there, the incursion became legitimate and even necessary.*

Because the intuition according to which something more important than the eternal return of the temptation to naturalize wage relations according to "competence" came to be confirmed, Marcelle, as a sociologist of labor, had a lot on her plate. When bosses today demand polyvalence, autonomy, responsibility, ability to learn, etc., they do not limit themselves to short-circuiting the qualifications that have been collectively negotiated, implying a diploma and seniority, they are demanding individual qualities, somewhat ineffable, but above all never recognized as acquired, qualities that must again and again be produced, demonstrated, and renewed. Workers will not rest on their laurels; they will have to be able to learn throughout their lives … if only to have

143

the good fortune to not end up unemployed. And the public authorities will take up the baton, in the name of the "information society." In schools, the content of knowledge will be defined as pretexts to train so-called transversal competencies. Thus, for example, history as "knowing how to situate oneself in time," and geography, of course, "in space." A poor food for those women who want more.

Marcelle Stroobants had a lot on her plate, but the "distance" required by her profession did not allow her to express what her letter vents: her anger and outrage toward the educational disaster. *Claiming to form an abstract competence, a competence abstracted from the situation that gives birth to it, is an enterprise that is not only pedagogically ineffective but also highly discriminatory. Methodology stripped of context, logic without history are so many spokes in the wheels for all those who don't have the opportunity to find elsewhere the meaning that shines by its absence.*

Can it really be competency to "know how to situate oneself in time?" If Marcelle can intervene in a question that cognitivist and pedagogical psychologists share, it is because she learned in the field, in industrial terrains, that qualification produces effects of competency, that workers who know themselves to be qualified succeed better than others, fresh from school with diplomas certifying general competencies, to learn how to use new machines. Whoever knows him/herself to be qualified, she had maintained in her thesis, is "empowered"— Marcelle uses the word "habilité", emphasizing the transformative efficacy of being authorized by oneself and by others to claim competence. The skill which you know, and are known, to have is neither a gift nor a dowry, that is, a social construction, a form of *habitus* that is received or interiorized, she writes us. It is a condition to confront what one doesn't know, to take risks, to learn. To become. And Marcelle tells us how, authorized by her field, she was able to ponder this question of "becoming competent." In her doctoral thesis, Marcelle

Stroobants put to work the concepts of the philosopher Gilbert Simondon:

How does one make a brick? asks Simondon. One needs a mold and clay, obviously, but neither the mold nor the clay has the power to explain the brick—only to arm the rivalry between those who invoke the power of the form and those who favor the material. Neither the clay nor the mold explains anything. On the contrary, it is what must be prepared, made compatible, so that the fabrication may succeed, that gives body to a brick, always this singular brick.

Neither gift nor dowry is sufficient to create singular competencies. It is only at the end of each episode of experience that the terms of this encounter separately appear as informal and formal knowledge, individual substances and social forms, materials and methods. With Simondon, Stroobants found the words to affirm that what is called the "transmission" of knowledge must, like the fabrication of the brick, be thought of in the manner of "hand-to-hand" combat. *One does not acquire competence in general; one "becomes" competent through hand-to-hand combat with what demands competence.*

The most surprising thing is not that schools are perpetually in crisis; it is that on occasion a good number of teachers succeed in forming seemingly competent students despite pedagogical ideas—that they occasionally share! No doubt, a good number of them fortunately do not refrain from cheating with the reforms, giving a boost in lessons of "learning to observe," getting students to discover there is something to understand, giving them food for thought.

When Marcelle Stroobants sent us this text, she answered, in her way, our request—here is the material, it's up to you to see if one can engage in an encounter with it, if you can make it compatible with your questions—which also means: it's up to you to see if what I did twenty years ago has something to do with what women are doing to thought.

Of course, and she couldn't help but know, these stories of the mold and the brick are full of meaning everywhere that the explanation of "culture" or socio-historical construction claims to be defined independently of "nature"—let's remember the perplexity of Mona Chollet. For Simondon, moreover, such explanatory styles amount to the eternal reprise of the old rivalry between form and material. The one who orders the bricks would like them to all be identical, explainable by the mold, and he will attribute any individuality—for him a defect—to the material. And the one who makes the brick will attribute the same individuality to his effort, through which the material is "informed," and will affirm that the "formation" is never done the same way twice. But these two rival explanations leave the individuation itself unspoken, the process by which a brick becomes. One is not born a woman, one becomes one, de Beauvoir wrote, but did she envision that this becoming could form the object of multiple appropriations, singular and collective, of a history of encounters with their coefficient of uncertainty and adventure?

Marcelle knows all this, and she also knows that the questions she thought she had to renounce when she accepted the constraints of the sociology of labor are, like those that make the girl climb upon the rooftop to escape the suffocating alternatives, questions that "wanted more"—"how does one become?" Thus, it could be said that Marcelle has been able to "create connections," as Benedikte Zitouni hopes her students will do. She had chosen disciplinary commitment, but she did not allow herself to be imprisoned in the lines of demarcation that transform this commitment into prohibitions arming wars of position—and so often causing interdisciplinary approaches to "fail," due to a lack of working on "compatibility." But Marcelle knows that as well.

What Marcelle could not know, on the other hand, is that her answer suggests to us a new version of the "we" that we fabulated, that of Virginia's unfaithful daughters. Fabulating "daughters," although unfaithful, "to Woolf," is this perhaps a question of empowerment? For it is affirming that Virginia Woolf was right, that the academic mold may have a fearsome power, but it's also a way for each one of us in our own way to bear witness to the fact that it doesn't have all the power. It is not that the brick making process has failed, it is simply that the produced bricks are not completely reliable, perfectly compliant, which is not at all the same thing.

Of course, each brick is singular in itself. We will not say that our male colleagues are all "true to the mold." On the other hand, we realize that our letter meant first of all to make a "certain type" of nonconformity perceptible. We can't keep ourselves from thinking that our male colleagues would not have dared to answer us, or would simply not have understood how we could incite them to what they would have seen as a somewhat indecent proposition, confounding private experience and intellectual life. The women who replied to us knew that the division between private and intellectual life, the "personal" and the "political" was not at all natural, that this division was part of the "mold."

However, if Marcelle's answer intervenes at the end of the journey, it is first of all because the question that she induced us to attribute to her, "what can you make of this?," is at this very moment ours as well. What can we do with all these departures from the norm? We know that these departures do not reveal a "truth"—they do not speak to a "feminine nature"—and their constellation is also not easily assimilated to a "specter" that would haunt the academic world—academia is perfectly able to accommodate that. They could remain as they are, without an epilogue, taken up as they are in adventures already undertaken. Can we do something else with them?

The answer does not belong to us, for, from now on, the "we" designates all those women who responded. It was time for us to meet.

EPILOGUE

> No easy unity is to be found on these matters, and no
> answers will make one feel good for long.

> Donna Haraway, *When Species Meet.*[1]

What are women doing to thought? Whoever
opened this book expecting an answer to this question
has obviously been disappointed. It has meaning
only to the extent that it created a meaning—a
fabulatory, speculative, ancestral one—for us and our
correspondents. And to the extent that it situated us,
that it authorized no generalization that might transcend
the process of taking up the baton. This is why we have
thought with women who, like ourselves, are engaged in
an academic journey and are, like ourselves, facing the
end of an epoch when the university had been able to
think of itself as a "place for thinking." Today, now more
than ever, we can remember that not only did Virginia
Woolf specifically caution her sisters against attempting
to make a career in the university, but, more generally,
against joining the procession of those who are engaged

---

1. Donna Haraway, *When Species Meet* (Minneapolis: University of Minnesota
Press, 2008), p. 41.

in these professions where it is a question of "making a career." Earn your living soberly, not a penny more than necessary, she had written, or else you will be trapped in this process that fabricates prostitutes defined by the competition for prestige, honors, and the devouring quest of a power that is always derisory, never sufficient.

Françoise Balibar reminded us that we are the heirs of the "republican" solution granted to the struggle of women, the heirs of the "universalist" (and meritocratic) perspective which replied to Woolf's *think we must* with a *think* they *may and can, just as we do. The* we *is obviously not the same. And we are the products of this situation. It is useless to tell ourselves fanciful stories: we think because "they" are willing us to, and because they have released us (partially, from 9 to 6) from our ancestral role (the fact that arriving at this point entailed struggling as women changes nothing in the historical process). Thus, if we think (we Belgian or French women), it cannot be in the same way as our grandmothers; we have been "assimilated."*

Is the (republican) mass over? We are undeniably "assimilated," considered "equivalent" from the point of view of the Republic. To reconsider the question of the mold and the brick, it could be said that in our case the attempt to ensure compatibility between the clay and the mold, now reputed to be "non-discriminatory," has produced a result deemed satisfactory, able to participate in the "edification of thought." And it's not a question of pleading a "different clay" for, as Marcelle Stroobants reminds us, to do that is to adopt the viewpoint of the master, he who proposes the mold. On the other hand, we can resist the idea that we are "finished products"— when it is a question of living beings, the process of creating compatibility is never finished.

Neither clay nor mold, neither gift nor dowry, and neither woman nor philosopher, Marcelle Stroobants writes to us, to which one will be able to add "neither assimilated nor unassimilated." And it is not only a question of refusing the categories that identify, but also of activating and keeping the space of hesitation open without which nothing can be fabricated. Here we take up the terms of Benedikte Zitouni, who insists that a difference be maintained between joining the procession of educated men and having access to the university. *For me this difference is very important, for in not making it, there is a risk of annihilating the moment of hesitation with a reaction of the sort: "Ah, OK, we are here now, Woolf's question is resolved, we no longer have the right to hesitate because women, now, whether we like it or not, are at the university, are already part of the system." Hesitation between "must we" or "must we not" go there? But also and more particularly, there is a hesitation and a difference to create between being there and joining the procession. You say that we are no longer in the time of Woolf. This is true, but not because women are now at the university and from this fact would all have joined the procession. We cannot register this fact that way. For me, if there is resonance between "then" and "now," it's precisely because this hesitation at the threshold of the university still exists and always will. And there are even some who turn their backs on the university and do their research elsewhere.*

No triumphalism here, no call to a sovereign freedom that would resist molding. Also no denunciation. To affirm that hesitation still exists and always will, to think that the situation is in tension, is not, cannot be identifying oneself with the victims, so numerous, who are judged improper, non compliant enough and rejected as "failures." This is why we must try to make that leitmotif of Donna Haraway our own: the non-innocence.[2] The search for an innocent position, that is typically, a victim's position, is, in our case at least, a veritable poison. In particular because it demands an impeccable, irreproachable victim, authorizing a clean cut in what is always *messy*, meaning both disorderly and dirty. As for us, one thing is certain, we cannot claim the "title" of victims, and we are certainly not irreproachable, nor can we define ourselves as thinking "in the presence

---

2. This leitmotif is found in *When Species Meet, ibid.*

151

of victims." Perhaps that happens to us, but it is certainly not what may give meaning to the question that makes us hesitate. It would thus give to our question the meaning of a crushing duty, not fabulatory, speculative, or ancestral. The affirmation of non-innocence—neither innocent nor guilty—is not moreover the (sad) recognition of a "fact." Such an affirmation has its own exigencies, and first is that of learning to situate oneself, and to do so in a way that creates new sensibilities, which better resist the alternatives that are deemed inescapable.

It is starting from the neither ... nor of non-innocence that we wish to experiment with the effects of characterizing the "we" of the unfaithful daughters of Virginia Woolf, whether they are at the university or occupy other professional positions, as "fusspots": those who have, more or less, benefitted from the republican offer—no discrimination, from now on you have the right to "do what we do," *as we do it*—but who don't feel bound to conform with loyalty to a now common order. Yes, we have accepted the benefits of the advantages reserved to those who are selected as deserving them. No, we are not victims of exclusion, of racism, of all the binaries that designate the abnormal or the pathological. But this does not commit us to the dignity that is called "not spitting in the soup," even when the taste of the soup is really bad. This does not commit us to not make a fuss, to "rationalize," to sigh "so it goes" when we see the working of a machine which differentiates those who win, from those who stagnate or who are eliminated Or when we rub shoulders with so many people ground down by abstract ideals that allow for the selection of the deserving ones, those who know how to play.

Women as liable to make a fuss are not heroic figures, rather they are damned nuisances. They don't accept, at least not completely, the place that has been made for them, and the silence that goes with it. They obtained the "right" to think from 9 to 6, like men—even if it means, according to the quasi norm of the double shift, taking

152

care of their children and their pots afterwards, but they lack gratitude toward those who have admitted them to their ranks. They do not let themselves, not completely, be assigned to the role to which they have acceded. And it is perhaps this refusal of assignation that constitutes one of the most remarkable themes of our inquiry.

We must be able to continue to hesitate, according to Benedikte Zitouni. *If you say to me "you philosophize like a woman," I answer, "no, I philosophize like a philosopher." If you say to me, "you philosophize like a philosopher," I answer, "but wait, perhaps I also philosophize a little like a woman." We may perhaps understand one another, but in any case, it's not assigned,* laughed Barbara Cassin during our meeting with our French correspondents in June 2010.

And here it is not a question of coming back to the great theme of feminine mystique, a sort of "negative feminology"—profane counterpart of a negative theology forbidding any positive formulation of the divinity. If it pleased Lacan to say that "nothing can be said about woman,"[3] that concerns him, and also perhaps concerns the type of ambition of knowledge that, he maintains, "woman" disappoints. But women often know how to find their way around with each other, if only to laugh, chatter, conspire, fulminate, they know how to find each other. The "you too, me too" proliferate the possible meanings and the versions, connecting them in multiple ways. Thus, in that month of June in Paris, the word "trickery" came up, that each woman had taken up, in jubilation, only to later decline it in more or less divergent styles, imposture, usurpation, a feeling of being mistaken for someone else, or the pleasure of the *trickster* practicing the art of escaping the attribution, "always and forever." Surprised and contagious laughter, with no need to compare or confront the versions. For what we felt at that moment was of the order of the creation of a

---

3. "Nothing can be said about woman," which he will take up again in *Encore*, with a Lacanian formula: "on la dit-femme, on la diffame." ("She is called woman, she is defamed.") Jacques Lacan, *Encore* (Paris: Seuil, 1998).

"ones" in the plural, or of a delocalized "we," all bearing repercussions and a certain lightness.

Discovering ourselves to be complicit in all these modalities that the theme of trickery evoked certainly could be assimilated into a reactive type of indulgence—a simple inversion with no scope other than transforming a common unease into a shared identity—again an assignation. Indeed it is a risk, but we know that such a risk is inherent in any operation of healing. The drugs that heal may have an inverse effect: they may become poison. What the Greeks called *pharmaka* demands an art of dosage, contrary to the Sovereign Good, which cannot harm, whose effects are, by definition, "innocent." But "to heal"—or more precisely, to *reclaim*[4]—recover, recuperate—demands this type of risk. The refusal which resonates as much in the permeability of Barbara as in the "thinking from hand to mouth" with which Woolf credits the history of women—a refusal of an assignation to think as an "assignation of residence," from 9 to 6 where one is professionally allowed to do so—only has meaning if the joy of thinking (even if it is painful) is recuperated. The lightness that we experienced in recognizing each other as "tricksters" demands, as Bernadette Bensaude-Vincent wrote to us, a new inversion. *If a "we" has suddenly surged from our meeting in Paris around a common feeling of being tricksters, because we felt "not in our place," I wonder if a we could also emerge from an inverse experience. The experience of feminine power. By this I mean the experience of no longer having to be a trickster in order to feel good,* in the right place, at the right moment. *Not by opportunism but by attention to the moment, listening to and decoding the background noise. To be able to act, operate, engage in several settings—from the*

---

4. This term, cultivated by American activists, is a witness to their filiation with feminist struggles. It combines the active and inventive themes of struggle and care. It is not only a question of recuperating what one has been separated from, but to "heal" the effects of that separation. It goes along with the necessity of learning to struggle without beginning to resemble, in the service of the cause, those against whom one is struggling—whatever the just and legitimate nature of that cause.

family to conferences, from courses to grading papers, from the kitchen to writing—without letting oneself be assigned a unique role, without incarnating a persona.

We know it well, we are far from having invented this laughter surprised at itself, this getting back to work in the mode of inversions, this experience that has the taste of a power, if it were activated, capable of troubling the seriousness of the assignations. We even think that such an experience accompanied and nourished movements that have engaged women for more than a century, and we can even imagine that those women who were persecuted in a more distant past, those witches meeting for rites that made men tremble, knew how to cultivate it. And perhaps we are touching on something that, once activated, once it makes the personal and the political communicate, brings or creates an answer to the question: "What are women doing to thought?"

However, what situates us is our very surprise when discovering together, each with the others and thanks to the others, that we who have accepted the republican offer are not feeling engaged by this acceptance. For this surprise also manifests a disconnection with a history that, even if we are indebted to it, is not really "ours." That is what Maria Puig de la Bellacasa stressed, after her reading of this manuscript: the voices that intertwine in the text, she writes to us, *spoke in isolation—yes, connected with some women, mothers, etc., but not with feminists.*

In fact, I believe that what pushes me away in part, from your manner of telling these stories, is that I feel heir to what those women made of their place, of their epoch, and to the movements this epoch was filled with [...]. I believe this is no doubt the reason that makes me incapable of immersing myself in your stories without feeling cut off from something. I don't see the interest *in giving such an importance to "thinking" as such. Perhaps I am too far away now, perhaps I am not a philosopher, perhaps I want to be a poet, like Leigh Star, but also like her other mother Adrienne Rich: in regard to the "woman question," I just am not/no longer able to think without the others who have thought "together" and through an epoch. For other questions, yes, I can do it […]. But for that one, for this question you pose, it's stronger than I, it's a* gut feeling of connection *that I can no longer evacuate—I have been profoundly transformed by my immersion in the collective history of feminism.* A shared pain and joy, *for our successes and failures. Even in the present isolation of my oh so Victorian house. Not one of your interlocutors seems to have felt the movement pass. Or in any case, that is not what they wanted to share—and don't tell me it's like that because it's the French speaking world! It's also the way of posing the question. You have chosen to pose it, in your letter, without that event of feminism. But to connect Woolf and today, with an event between the two, the democratization of access … the fact that we are there […].*

It's not a problem, it's just another manner of doing things, another point of departure, as if you needed to talk right now about something, and needed to make this journey together, whereas for me, it is not the right moment to talk like this. Perhaps my question, if there is one that I'm burning to ask today, is what to do, now, in order to prolong the history of feminisms by not evacuating its difficulties and pitfalls but by lugging around its explosions and internal implosions in one's heart—why indeed have so many of these women decided to no longer refer to this history?

Maria Puig's question needs to be heard, and even more so, as she stresses, because a book, this book we're working on, *is something public, situated, and that has effects which are tied to an epoch.* But it cannot be a question of either explaining or justifying ourselves. Rather: to acknowledge. For some among us, feminism has had, or still has, a great importance, but what Maria speaks about is the attachment to a concrete milieu, to stories, to successes, to heartbreaks that we have not experienced, or only through hearsay. Neither have we had, as a milieu for thought, what are called *studies*, and we are not particularly proud of our "provincialism," of our relative ignorance of what the francophone university

156

world incites us to ignore. Even if these *studies (gender, queer, cultural, post-colonial, critical,* and even *French*) do not really correspond to the transformation of the modes of production of knowledge for which feminists have struggled, Barbara Cassin writes us, she is among those who, *here, now, in France, at the CNRS, are trying to establish* gender studies *against all odds.* And Benedikte Zitouni adds that, *in fact, when one has not been part of it—which is my case—there is the necessity to fabricate a position vis-à-vis this field. Overall, I need* gender studies *but what is the link that I can claim with these* studies *when moreover, I don't work on the "corpus" so to speak? I now call myself an amateur of* gender studies *when I speak, for example, about the text on situated knowledge by Donna Haraway.*

"A little late," some women will perhaps say, and with reason. But especially as an "amateur," without that *gut feeling* of belonging in a collective history, to which Maria bears witness. We know that, when we read Haraway in particular, we are profiting from a shared experience of joy and sorrow, without having paid the price, without having struggled, hoped, risked, dared to scandalize like those women with whom she has shared so many stories, explosions and implosions. We read her without necessarily reading the women writers to whom she constantly refers; we are abstracting her from the "corpus" that she keeps on weaving. There is no excuse for that because it would transform belonging into an abstract ideal. The fact is that not one among us had these women writers as privileged interlocutors in her journey of thought. For each one of us, what thinking meant was learned in a world of men.

However, in order to prolong the collective adventure of feminisms, is it necessary to lug around in our hearts the living memory of its explosions and internal implosions? We don't know, and the theme of taking up the baton that preoccupies us doesn't tell us. What we know is that taking up the baton is never innocent and we only hope that none of those who live with this memory will turn it into an inescapable reference which we would betray, will seek to make us feel guilty, or to unmask us as imposters. After all, even Malinche, the collaborator par excellence, who, as a companion to Cortez, was his translator and his advisor in his dealings with the Mexican people, became for Mexicans the mother of an irreversibly mixed-race people who can no longer dream of purity. And she has become, through the intervention of women of color in the feminist movements in the United States, the one who, rather than dying with dignity, made the choice to survive, even betray her origins, that is to say, the one who questioned all pretensions of innocence. For us, she recalls Barbara Cassin's mother facing the Germans who came to arrest her husband—*when it is necessary, when it's a question of life or death, women excel....* But, writes Donna Haraway in her *Cyborg Manifesto*, she is also the one who mastered the language of the conqueror, and "hints at the possibility of world survival not because of her innocence, but because of her ability to live on the boundaries, to write without the founding myth of original wholeness."[5]

That we may have accepted the "republican" offer without feeling engaged by the abstraction of an amnesiac equality that it implies certainly doesn't make us one of those "transgressive" figures who along with Malinche haunt the pages of the *Cyborg Manifesto*. However, each time that we feel capable of indifference or humor in relation to inescapable alternatives, each time that we succeed in multiplying the versions rather than submitting to the one that gives us a choice "either this ... or that," we know that we make teeth grind, that we enervate those who live in the foundation myth of thought: the noble revolt of Socrates against those sophists who were playing with words and disconcerting those who, seriously and with integrity, were seeking which truth to submit themselves to.

5. Donna Haraway, *Simians, Cyborgs and Women: the Reinvention of Nature* (New York: Routledge, 1991), p. 176.

But here Maria Puig's objection resonates: *I do not see* the interest *in giving such importance to "thinking" as such*—as well as to those who live "this founding myth of thought." From the beginning, we made the choice to address ourselves to women for whom, we supposed, the question "how to think?" matters as such. Did we succeed in learning, in the course of this journey, something that would be worthy of interesting others, worthy of giving ideas, that is to say, appetite, to those women (and perhaps men) who will read this book and who have too often been convinced that "thinking" is not for them? Have we succeeded in bringing to life a "twelfth camel" that gives our question the ability to get out of the first circle, the one of women who could accept that this question might concern them?

Barbara Cassin writes to us, *my twelfth camel is my relation to languages.* But if her relation is that of a *trickster*, if she loves the ability of words to trip up those who want to fix them firmly in the service of truth, if she cultivates homonymy for its power to make translations diverge and proliferate that are the most promising or the least expected ones, it is not, or not only, for pleasure. When she defends a relativism oriented not toward the truth, but toward the search for the better, Cassin has a gravity that reminds us of Haraway. The woman philosopher is not the itching powder of the male, which keeps him from sleeping or reactivates the watchfulness of his Thought. The figure of the Hysteric, who always wants more and makes men think, this definition of what women would do to thought, is again an assignation. Perhaps the worst of all for it captures the refusal of the assignation. *The idea that one would produce objects that trouble the great philosophy is what kills me.* We are dealing with an entirely different question, the idea of a world that could be habitable. A world where Socrates would no longer torpedo, would no longer plunge the unhappy inhabitants of Athens into perplexed stupidity, discovering that they don't know "what" they say, a world where Mary, the kitchen maid, the children of Abdallah and the Duke of Devonshire would find pleasure in exploring bifurcations, encounters and divergences, which every word is liable to prompt, without seeking to bring them back to reason. In response to Mary's question, wondering if the master has gone mad, Cassin proposes to us, what, for Francis Ponge, "understanding a word" would demand, or "understanding each other," between a metaphysician and a cook.

Each word has many habits and powers; each time it would be necessary to care for them all, to use them all. This would be the height of the "adequacy of terms." But each word is obscure if it veils a corner of the text, if it fascinates like a star, if it is too radiant.

It would be necessary in the phrase that the words which compose it be in such places that the phrase has a meaning for each of the meanings of each one of its terms. This would be the height of the "logical depth of the phrase" and really the "life" through the infinite multiplicity and the necessity of relations.

That is to say that this would be the height of pleasure of reading for a metaphysician. And the cook would find it pleasant in her own way. Or understand it. The rule of pleasing would thus be obeyed as much as possible, or the desire to please satisfied.

In our regions, it is standard practice, to treat "politically correct" language with derision, and to identify it as thought terrorism made in the U.S.A. And, perhaps, the rule and the desire to please are in fact not always well served by the constraints of this language. The women who have struggled so that people learned to hear what words said, at first thought of their power to humiliate, to debase, to kill, not of the poetic power to connect without uniting. And it is there that we can seize the testing character of the poet's proposition, its own way to be "correct." For the desire, the rule to please can offend the women whom this world angers, or enrages, those for whom forgetting this rage would be to betray the children of Abdallah and Mary, the kitchen maid, and to seduce the Duke who loves poetry. Isn't that moreover what we have done, together, women benefitting from the possibilities of the culture—thinking together, forgetting the excluded, both men and women? And here again is the feeling of guilt. But Mary, the children of Abdallah and these girls who wanted more, evoked by Zitouni, do they need this rage?

Mary loves stories, and Abdallah's children living in the suburbs of our towns, would perhaps like stories besides those that too often take them as hostages in theoretical conflicts. Their life is now, and they are not demanding that we admit our guilt, or they demand it and our confessions poison them—something more is necessary, for the confession does not nourish. And we would really like our famous culture to make us able to recount other stories which, perhaps, would be worthy of pleasing them. Worthy of evoking, fabulous hope, the possibility of exploring words and worlds together, with their ability both to wound and damage, their power to connect one's life and the infinite and necessary multiplicity of relations.

"Women are unpredictable. Everything seems to be going well, and suddenly they get all worked up. Someone says one word, perhaps a bit unfortunate, and they make a big fuss!" Perhaps that was the reaction of educated men while reading *Three Guineas*, that aggressive pamphlet written by a woman writer whose writing was usually so "pleasant." And if it was necessary to seek not an answer—ridicule doesn't kill, they say, but all the same!—but a type of working hypothesis that ties the question of what women are doing to thought with what we learned in the course of these several months of speculation, laughter, anger, doubt, perplexity, it would be in that direction that we would like to go. For it is not a question of forgetting anger or sorrow. Certainly, we would not wish to sacrifice the pleasure of thinking, of inventing, of proliferating stories, because our stories can only ratify the inhabitable character of the world if

161

they are devoid of pleasure and invention. But sorrow and anger are never very far away, and when they spring up we sometimes make a fuss. This often produces confusion for others but also for the one who may well ask herself "what possessed me," without really regretting it. However, if it must be a question of "doing" something to thought, this springing up and the utter confusion that it may incite are not sufficient. One only "does" if one learns to do, for oneself and collectively.

Benedikte and Barbara, notably, seem to us to have learned to transform their anger into strength— and their example shows us that it is not a question of placing oneself at a reflexive distance, of mastery or of instrumentalism. Rather of an art: they know how to make a fuss without the confusion turning against them and making them a target for explanation—she has her moods, ah hormones! And the example that Laurence Bouquiaux gave us speaks of what a collective apprenticeship could mean, able to contribute to the stories of what "women do to thought." It may be that the time of being angry together will come again, but we may learn to listen to the resurgence of a sudden recalcitrance—to not be astonished, to not look for explanations, and especially to not try to appease, to not yield to the temptation to play the role of mediator. Rather, be ready to take up the baton, in your own style, to seize and throw in supplementary reasons—and there are always supplementary reasons—for which the situation may in effect elicit recalcitrance.

An art must be cultivated, and it demands trust, but a strange type of trust—not in oneself, "I know what I do," but rather in the situation and what it demands. The question is especially not one of Truth, or of redemption. We know well that we have already tolerated what, in this case, has elicited anger, and we know that we will tolerate it again. The very strength of women who make a fuss is to not represent the True, rather to be witnesses for the possibility of other ways of doing what would perhaps be "better." The fuss is not the heroic statement of a grand cause, in the name of which sacrifice would be *de rigueur*, it instead affirms the need to resist the stifling impotence created by the "no possibility to do otherwise, whether we want it or not," which now reigns everywhere.

It may very well reign everywhere, but when it concerns the university, the temptation exists to not make a fuss. After all, the fact that those who profited from what so many others were excluded from—as if that was their just due, as if it were merited—have been incapable of resisting the destruction of their world, the submission to the "no possibility to do otherwise" could well correspond to what is called "immanent justice." Haven't we merited this, we the meritorious ones? But the lights are flashing red. Women who make a fuss have nothing to do with merit. On the other hand, they have learned that, in our lives and in our worlds, it is always by profiting from a weakness, from a carelessness, from an inertia, from a cowardice that the logic of the "no possibility" is put in place ... and murmurs to us that we have merited what happens to us, that the least we can do is accept it, with dignity, without making a fuss.

But this murmur is perhaps that of our epoch, inhabited as it is by the shame of having let it happen, of not succeeding in resisting. And perhaps the question that we sought to pose from our own terrain, the university, could echo elsewhere without taking anywhere the posture of innocence. Everywhere the question of resisting this shame is insisting, everywhere the "what happened to us?" must fabricate thought, that is to say, one will have understood, life and not complaints and resentment.

Our working hypothesis on the subject of what women could do to thought is therefore both modest and ambitious, and it is not at all polemical. It is modest because it does not set the stage for "another thought," which we don't know from where we would pull it, since, we have said, our own thought was fabricated in a world of men.

But it is ambitious, as each time it is a question of transmuting into a strength what usually is designated as a frowned upon and somewhat embarrassing behavior.

And it is not polemical, because its origin is rooted in perplexity, that perplexity Benedikte knew how to make resonate so well when she wondered *how can they believe that we are so ignorant?* A perplexity in regard to what makes men "keep going," the "grandeur" that commands that they hold on. To this question, responses of the psychoanalytic type have certainly been offered, but we don't want to interpret because this grandeur, which has no doubt been why they can be trusted to go to the front and to possible death without making too much fuss, we want nothing else but to demoralize it.

Virginia Woolf doubted that women could make a difference in the places of knowledge where they were admitted from that point on. Françoise Balibar echoes this by saying that the difference is not perceptible, but she does it with the diagnostic of what one could call a general sadness (*everyone would like to work less ...*).

A helpless sadness, which characterizes the manner in which we are meant both to define the situation and to respond to it. We may hold on, or break down, but we have to ensure everyone maintains with dignity the course toward a future which no longer has a future.

What if the stability of this course required this anticipated, sad dignity? What if the difference a hypothetical relaying of fussy, undignified behavior could make, was an unknown of the situation? Would this be a possible gift from the marked gender to all, men and women, who are marked for zombification?[6] Learning to make a fuss, taking up the baton of the fusses that others make is not a proposition addressed

6. See Suzanne Ryan, "Academic Zombies: A Failure to Resist or a Means of Survival?" in Australian Universities Review, vol. 54, no. 2 (2012), pp. 3-11 (online).

only to women, even if the courageous dignity of those who know the importance of not making it, belongs to male virtues. The question of women making a fuss is addressed to all women and all men, in the same manner as the question of a habitable world: a world just a little better, not the world where Good, however it is defined, would have triumphed over evil.

Execution of Georgette Thomas, place d'Armes in Romorantin.
(Le Journal illustré, July 6, 1887)

Here, one could snicker—and you believe that in making a fuss, you are going to be able to resist, to thwart what is devastating our worlds? We don't believe anything, we simply know that it would be better to do so rather than courageously submit, with dignity, to what is presented as inescapable. And we would like to conclude by addressing a thought to a particular woman who, because she knew how to make a fuss, to thrash about, to scream, and cry, saved the life of many. Georgette Thomas was condemned with her husband for the murder of his helpless mother, who, they believed, was bewitched and whom they threw in the hearth fire, thinking they could escape the bad luck that hounded them. She had to be carried to the guillotine by the assistant executioner, completely lacking the dignified courage that, it seems, creates the grandeur of men who climb up the scaffold—a courage which also makes the position of executioner tolerable. Following her execution, on January 24, 1887, it is said that Louis Deibler, the chief executioner, asked the President of the Republic to automatically grant clemency to women, these spoilers of his profession. That was the case until Vichy.[7] Women persisted—in 1947, Lucienne Fournier, who had thrown her husband over a bridge on the Marne, the evening of their wedding, had to be dragged from her cell to the scaffold. She urinated from fear and screamed, "I didn't do anything!" She was the next to the last. Women, decidedly, were unworthy of the supreme punishment, incapable of "paying their debt to society." May their examples give us the strength to not submit ourselves with dignity.

---

7. Élisabeth Ducourneau, guillotined in 1941, had thought that her appeal for clemency had been accepted by Pétain, as was the tradition. When they announced to her that the moment had come to pay her debt to society, she is said to have responded: "But certainly, sir, I have some money in the Clerk of Court's office...." The execution was very painful.

Univocal Publishing
123 North 3rd Street, #202
Minneapolis, MN 55401
www.univocalpublishing.com

ISBN 9781937561192

Jason Wagner, Drew S. Burk
(Editors)
All materials were printed and bound
in March 2014 at Univocal's atelier
in Minneapolis, USA.

This work was composed in Futura and Meridien.
The paper is Mohawk Via, Pure White Linen.
The letterpress cover was printed
on Neenah's Classic Crest, Tarragon.
Both are archival quality and acid-free.